AF292256

SHERRIE LEVINE
HONG KONG DOMINOES

David Zwirner Books

Brazilian Ex Voto Figure: 1, 2019
Cast bronze
11 × 2 ¾ × 2 ⅜ inches
27.9 × 7 × 6 cm

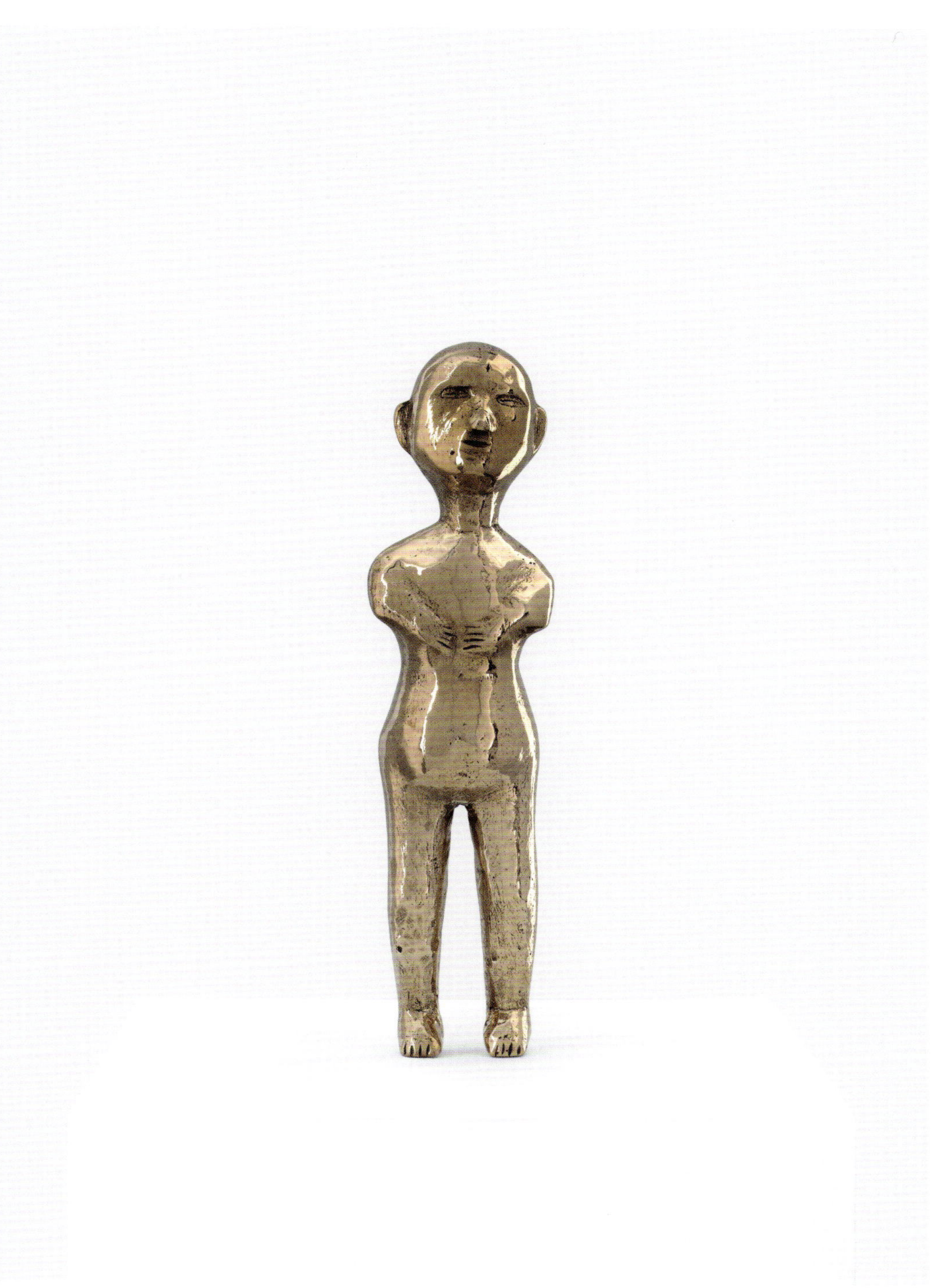

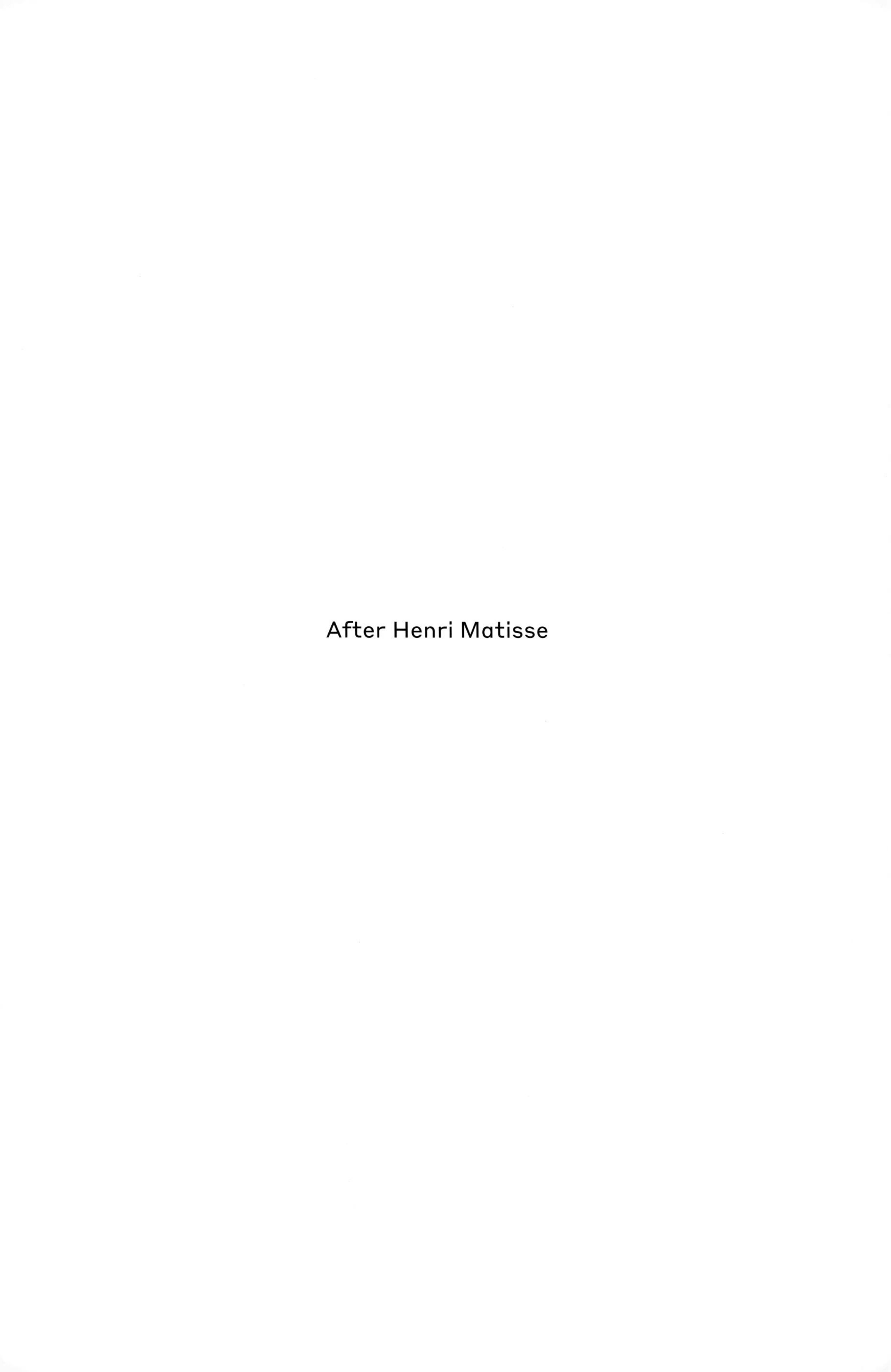

After Henri Matisse

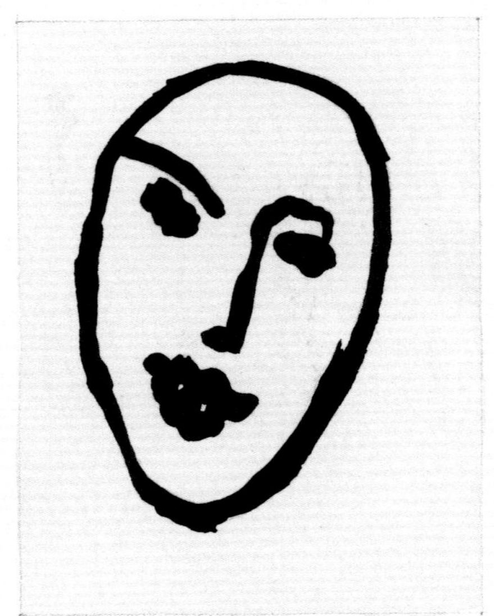

After Henri Matisse: 1, 1985
Graphite, watercolor, and wash on paper
14 × 11 inches
35.6 × 27.9 cm

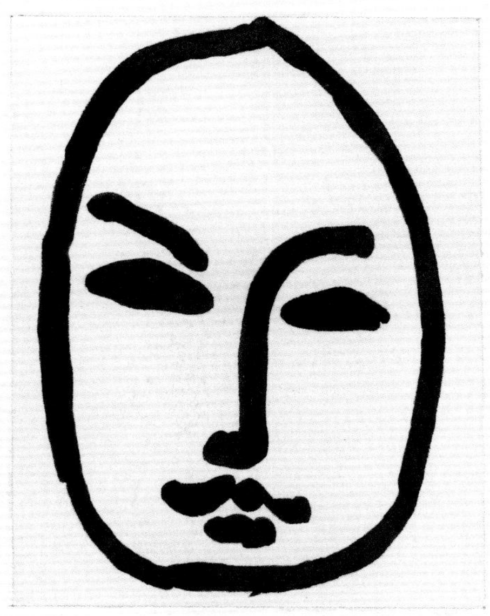

After Henri Matisse: 5, 1985
Graphite, watercolor, and wash on paper
14 × 11 inches
35.6 × 27.9 cm

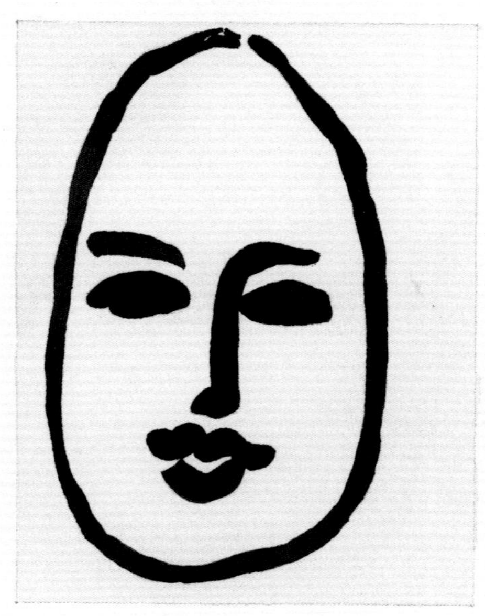

After Henri Matisse: 6, 1985
Graphite, watercolor, and wash on paper
14 × 11 inches
35.6 × 27.9 cm

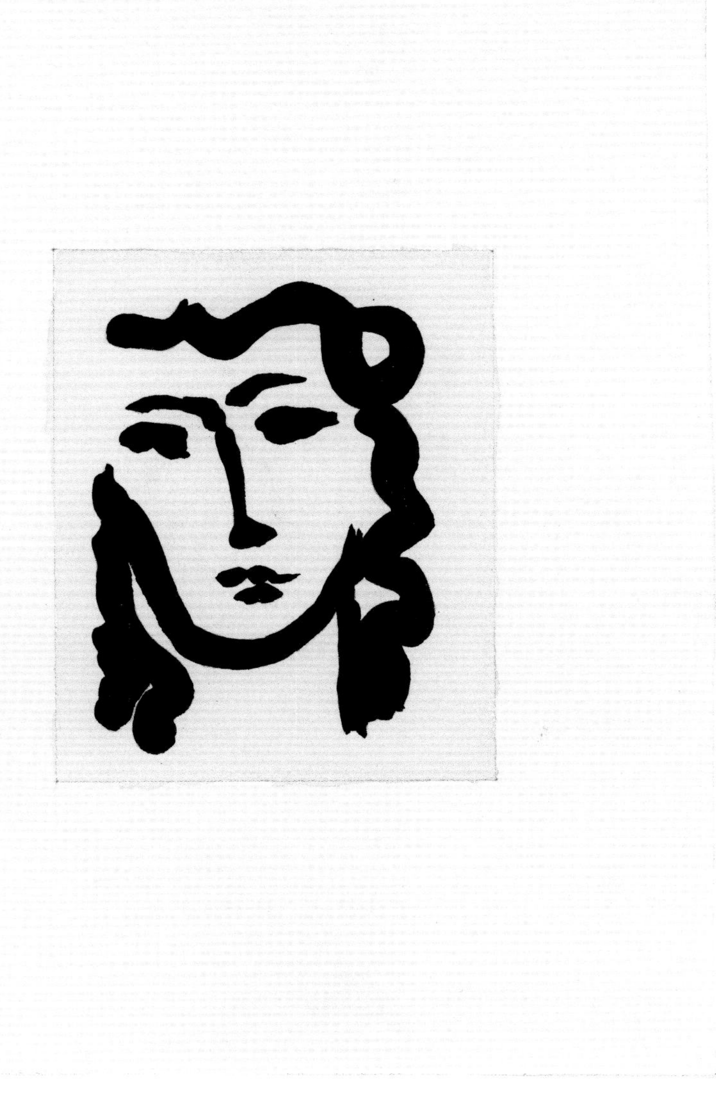

After Henri Matisse: 12, 1985
Graphite, watercolor, and wash on paper
14 × 11 inches
35.6 × 27.9 cm

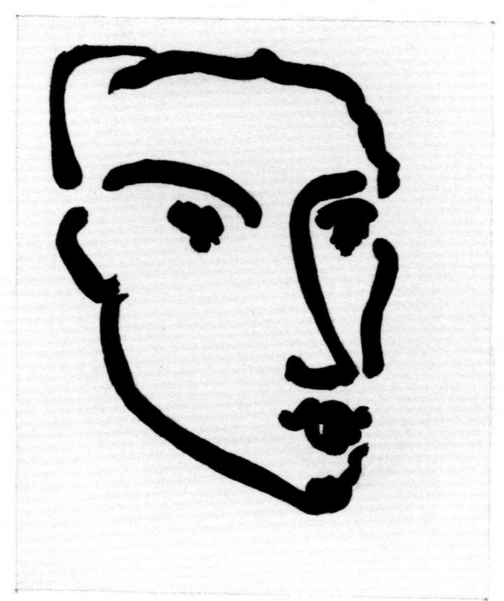

After Henri Matisse: 14, 1985
Graphite, watercolor, and wash on paper
14 × 11 inches
35.6 × 27.9 cm

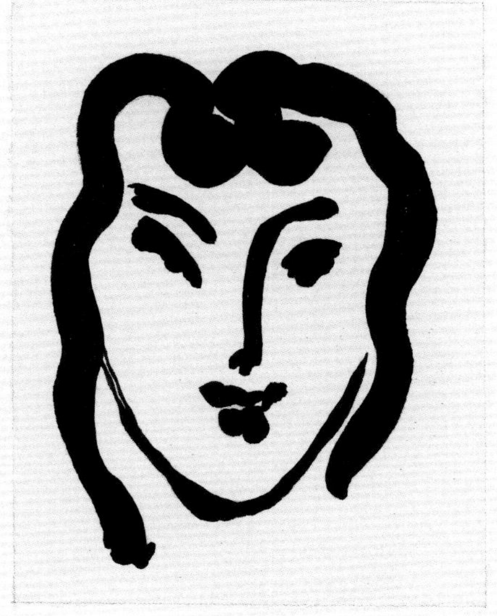

After Henri Matisse: 15, 1985
Graphite, watercolor, and wash on paper
14 × 11 inches
35.6 × 27.9 cm

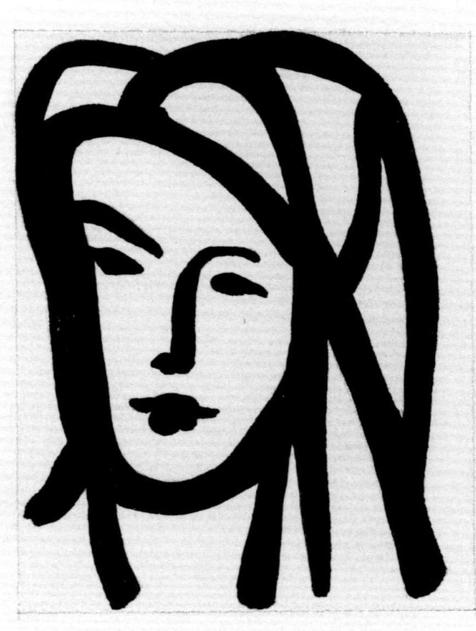

After Henri Matisse: 16, 1985
Graphite, watercolor, and wash on paper
14 × 11 inches
35.6 × 27.9 cm

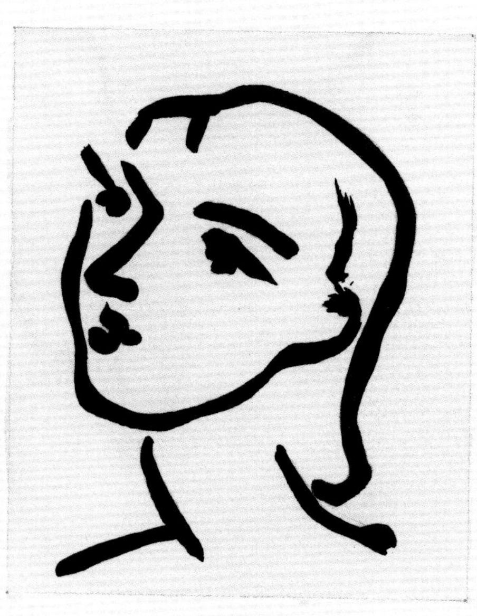

After Henri Matisse: 17, 1985
Graphite, watercolor, and wash on paper
14 × 11 inches
35.6 × 27.9 cm

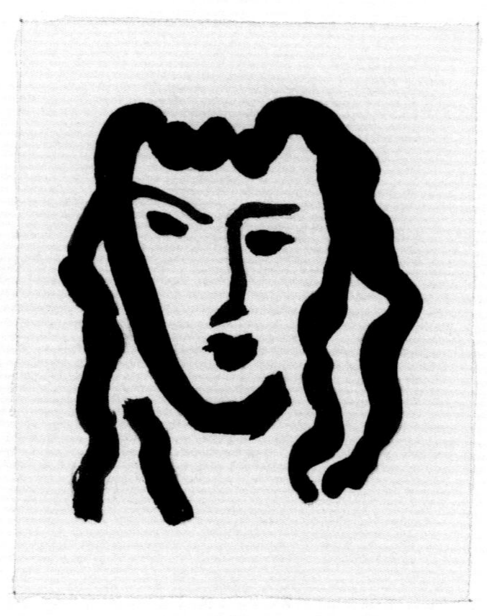

After Henri Matisse: 18, 1985
Graphite, watercolor, and wash on paper
14 × 11 inches
35.6 × 27.9 cm

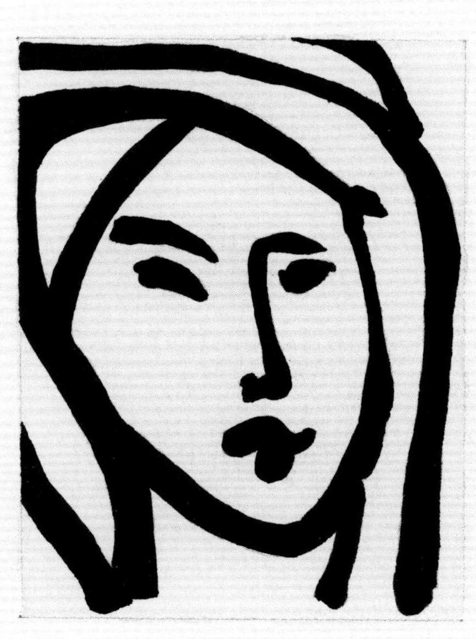

After Henri Matisse: 19, 1985
Graphite, watercolor, and wash on paper
14 × 11 inches
35.6 × 27.9 cm

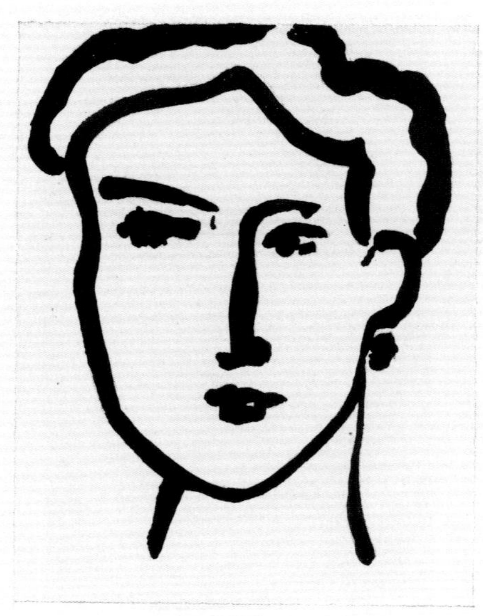

After Henri Matisse: 20, 1985
Graphite, watercolor, and wash on paper
14 × 11 inches
35.6 × 27.9 cm

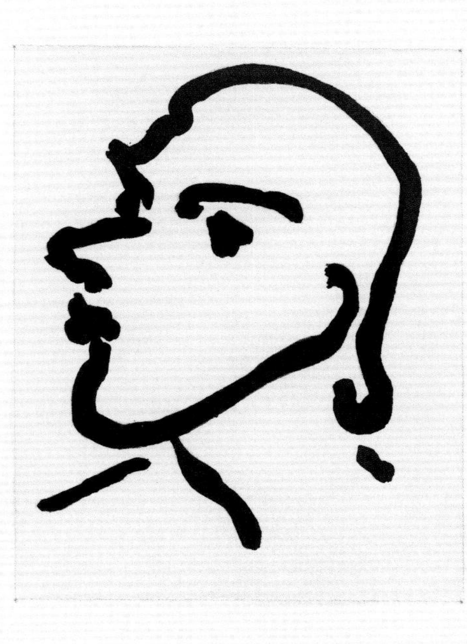

After Henri Matisse: 21, 1985
Graphite, watercolor, and wash on paper
14 × 11 inches
35.6 × 27.9 cm

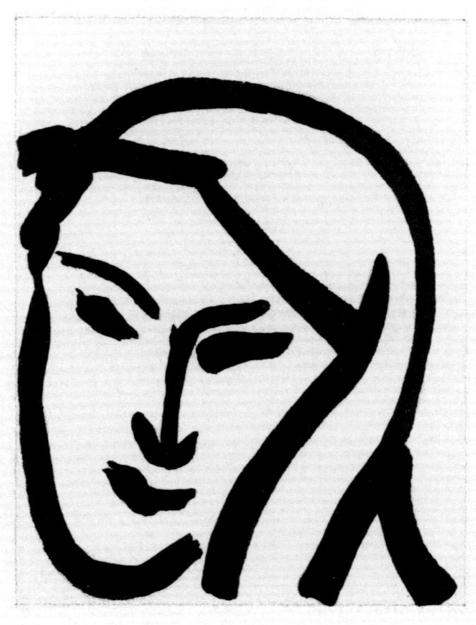

After Henri Matisse: 24, 1985
Graphite, watercolor, and wash on paper
14 × 11 inches
35.6 × 27.9 cm

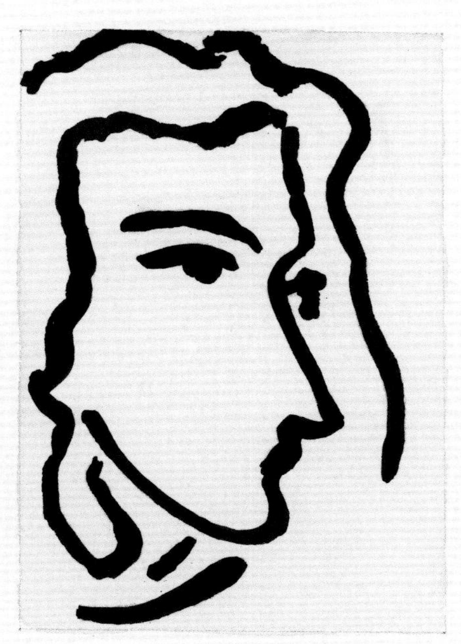

After Henri Matisse: 27, 1985
Graphite, watercolor, and wash on paper
14 × 11 inches
35.6 × 27.9 cm

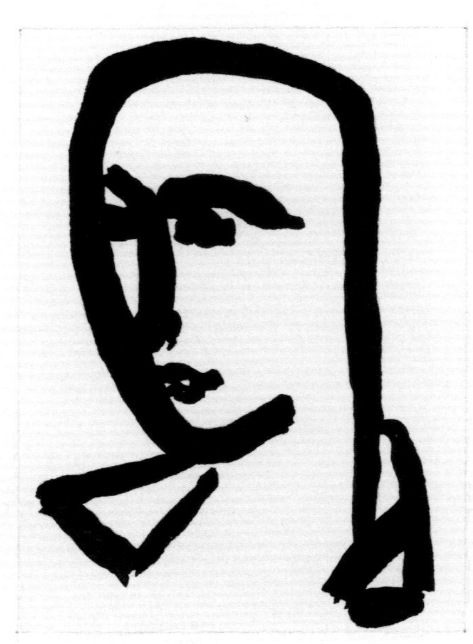

After Henri Matisse: 36, 1985
Graphite, watercolor, and wash on paper
14 × 11 inches
35.6 × 27.9 cm

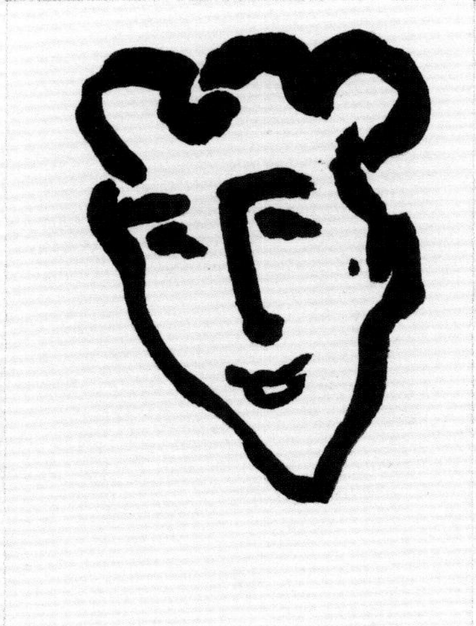

After Henri Matisse: 37, 1985
Graphite, watercolor, and wash on paper
14 × 11 inches
35.6 × 27.9 cm

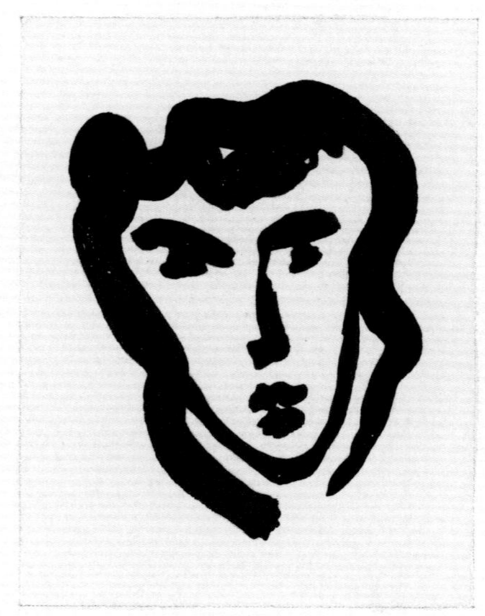

After Henri Matisse: 38, 1985
Graphite, watercolor, and wash on paper
14 × 11 inches
35.6 × 27.9 cm

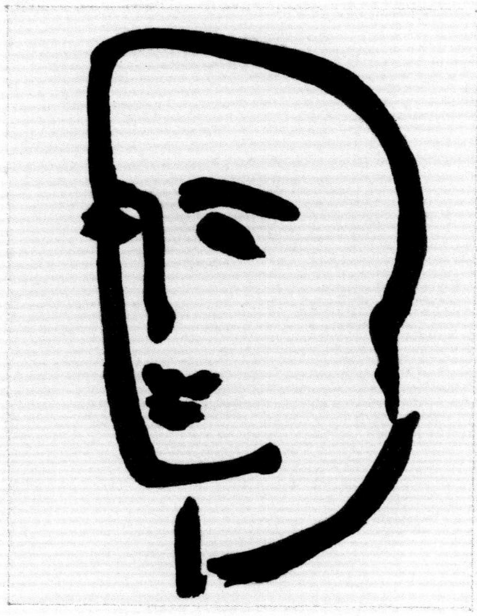

After Henri Matisse: 39, 1985
Graphite, watercolor, and wash on paper
14 × 11 inches
35.6 × 27.9 cm

Sherrie Levine: Take a Picture to Make a Picture
Larry List

From her 1977 New York debut in the group show *Pictures*, at Artists Space,[1] to the present, Sherrie Levine has drawn inspiration from art-historical and anthropological sources to create work that challenges traditionally held ideas about authorship, ownership of ideas, and fixity of identity.

From 1965 to 1973, Levine attended the University of Wisconsin–Madison, a hotbed of radical political action against the Vietnam War. Her formative environment was one in which students were actively taking over by staging protests and challenging authority. Hence she has long felt a natural kinship with the early twentieth-century Dada movement, which formed to challenge the authority of European academic art and society in reaction to the violence and insanity of World War I.

Her cast-bronze *Hobby Horse* (2014; pp. 46–49) is an iconic reference to the Dadaists, in that "hobby horse" is the English translation of the French word "dada," which was chosen at random from a French–German dictionary to become the art movement's name.[2] Seemingly simple and straightforward, like a Trojan horse, this shiny bronze work draws the viewer in, yet it embodies Levine's and the Dadaists' passion for contradiction and confounding easy interpretations. Like two parallel trains of thought, the two rocker elements of *Hobby Horse* are firmly fixed to the body of the work, but each moves in radically different curvatures and would throw off any potential rider—just as readily as anyone expecting a "smooth ride" and one consistent interpretation of Levine's work will surely be thrown off.

Dadaist fellow-traveler Marcel Duchamp provided inspiration to Levine as well. His creation of readymades—the common, everyday objects chosen by the artist and elevated to the status of artworks simply by his choice and signature—empowered Levine to adapt a deadpan "take a picture to make a picture" embrace of industrial photo-reproduction techniques while still in graduate school.

Enrolled not as a painter or sculptor but as a printmaker, she learned to use a copy camera and commercial offset presses and became proficient at photo-lithography, photo-silkscreen, and photo-etching techniques. Her printmaking background made it natural for her to think in terms of generating multiple copies of an identical image, working

in series of related images, and producing multiple variations
of a type of image in different sizes and materials.

Working in commercial art studios in Madison, she grew
familiar with the idea that anybody's artwork—a drawing,
painting, or object—could readily be altered, rephotographed,
resized, and converted to any other print media for final
display.[3] "I was really interested in how they [commercial artists]
dealt with the idea of originality. If they wanted an image,
they'd just take it. . . . There was no sense that images belonged
to anybody; all images were in the public domain and as an
artist I found that very liberating."[4] Hence her practice became
one of choosing, reproducing, and re-presenting images and
objects as her own artworks, challenging accepted notions of
authorship and ownership of images and ideas.

In Duchamp's assumption of an alternate, opposite sex
identity, Rrose Sélavy, Levine saw another way to challenge
authority and gain a new form of creative freedom, even from
Duchamp. "Like most women, I'd gotten pretty tired of being
depicted and represented by men"[5] and so she declared that
"what I like to imagine I'm doing, in the realm of the symbolic,
of course, is dismantling the bachelor machine [of Duchamp's
Large Glass]."[6] From that early point in her career, Levine
assumed a long series of alternate, opposite sex identities by
appropriating the works of male artists and stereotypically
"male subjects," such as her *After Feininger* series (2021; pp.
90–103) of eleven industrial or architectural sites in the midst
of otherwise beautiful, monumental natural surroundings.
Though described by Douglas Crimp as "scenes of nature that
are utterly familiar,"[7] each image depicts man's intrusion
or despoiling of the vast American landscape. Although the
majority of the Bauhaus architect-turned-photographer
Andreas Feininger's work was done in black and white for *LIFE*
magazine, Levine chose eleven images that reflect Feininger's
most technically up-to-date work—all in color, since he had
published an influential textbook *Basic Color Photography* in
1972 that Levine may have encountered during her school
years. For Levine, who usually works in even-numbered series,
this odd number of images and mixture of horizontal and
vertical formats, if kept in sequence, will result, like the *Hobby
Horse* ride, in an asymmetric, or unbalanced, experience no
matter how they're arranged.

Another typically male subject that Levine has addressed
is the female nude, as in her *Monochromes After Renoir Nudes*
series (2016; pp. 52–77). Just as the twentieth-century

sculptor Constantin Brancusi sought to reduce a natural form to its essence in sculpture by idealizing it, in her *Monochromes After Renoir Nudes* works, Levine sought the same goal by employing twenty-first-century digital means. Levine isolated the female figure in each Renoir work and then used a chromatic computer algorithm to calculate each figure's average color, resulting in a unique and specific "essence"— a modernist monochrome panel.

Also as early as her graduate studies, Levine began to experiment with the German concept of *Maskenfreiheit*, the transformative shamanistic freedom offered by wearing a mask. This idea works in tandem with her underlying assumption of alternate male artist identities. Showcased in this volume are examples of Levine's delicate *After Henri Matisse* series of watercolors (1985; pp. 8–25), each one gently isolating, transforming, and freeing the face of one of Matisse's models from its master. In retrospect, these intimately scaled, carefully chosen, and well-controlled watercolors stand in sharp contrast to the large, bombastic neo-expressionistic stylings of fellow artists Julian Schnabel, Francesco Clemente, and Sandro Chia, and the sardonic life-size sinking bronze *Lifeboat* and floating basketball works of Jeff Koons.

In line with her early printmaking conditioning to explore variations of an idea in different sizes and materials, Levine continued her *Maskenfreiheit* with photo series of works picturing masks, such as *After Edward Curtis: 1–5* (2005) and *African Masks After Walker Evans: 1–24* (2014) and her series of bronze casts of Japanese Tengu, Nepalese Citipati, African Lega, and other tribal masks.

In these and her cast-bronze *Brazilian Ex Voto Figure* (2019; p. 5), Levine exemplifies another characteristic of the Dada artists—a fetishizing interest in the alchemical, whereby she transposes the original source objects made of humble base materials such as wood or clay into "noble" materials such as polished bronze. Not only does she practice the art of the readymade by elevating these worldly objects into the timeless realm of art through her choice, but she also transforms them from perishable objects into permanent objects through transmuting them into another material, memorializing each object of ritual transformation or creative disruption.

Levine's *Hong Kong Dominoes: 1–12* (2017; pp. 80–87) embody two of the artist's central interests: the freedom afforded by wearing a mask or disguise, and the freedom offered by engaging in play, an activity with no worldly purpose but amusement and pleasure. *The Probert Encyclopaedia of Mythology* identifies a domino as "a kind of hood worn by the canons of a cathedral church . . . and later . . . a mourning-veil for women, and later still as a half-mask worn by women when travelling or at a masquerade, for disguise."[8] With her career-long interest in pairs, duplicates, copies, and assumed identities, Levine may have been inspired to duplicate her *Hong Kong Dominoes* panels by the Rudyard Kipling poem "Pink Dominoes," from 1922, about the mistaken identities of two identically dressed ladies at a masquerade ball.

While her work lends itself to many conceptual interpretations, Levine has stated her belief that "it's more useful to think of art-making as play rather than work. Fantasies of aggression and control have an interesting place there. I think that's one of the reasons that I've been so attracted to games as subject matter."[9] As subject matter for Levine's work, dominoes are ideal: they are not one game but a family of games with a multitude of variant forms,[10] made of many different materials, and with varying numbers of component parts. Typically small black or white oblong tablets twice as long as they are wide, divided in half with dice-like dots numbering between one and six on each half, dominoes are highly abstract but visually graphic. They represent a center of social and communal play yet, in some variants, the games can be highly competitive and require complex mathematic calculations, demanding a combination of skill and chance.

Here, grouped in unbounded clusters of eight, to fill her favored twenty-by-sixteen-inch panel format, the domino dots suggest early computer key punch cards or harken back to the even earlier program cards of Jacquard looms. Like dominoes, the looms are "a 'chain of cards' . . . laced together into a continuous sequence. Multiple rows of holes are on each card, with one complete card corresponding to one row of the design."[11]

Shown in Hong Kong, they have special resonance inasmuch as dominoes did not appear in Italy and France until the eighteenth century but may have been in play as early as the Southern Song period (1127–1279) in China.[12] The left half of each panel, top and bottom, even mimics the line from the eighth-century poem "Grievances of a Spring Maiden," describing a "plum blossom tree in front of the white jade hall." Each top five and ace represents the plum blossom tree while the two columns of six below symbolize the jade hall.[13] Like Levine's ganging of eight dominoes together in one panel, the game of *pu pai* (laying out dominoes) requires players to make the most interesting combinations of each group of eight pieces they draw.[14]

Duchamp attempted to integrate the game of chess, its logic and imagery, into fine art as a genre equal to landscape, figuration, and still life. In Levine's case, her treatment of an array of game board motifs is one of the only areas of her work predicated upon the appropriation of an entire collective genre of patterns or design, not just one individual artist's work at a time.

The complex grid patterns of her game boards and pieces, including her *Lead Chevron* backgammon patterned series (1987), *Lead Checks and Chevron* backgammon and chessboard grid series (1987–1988), *After Duchamp: Chessboards* chessboard grid series (1989–1990), and *Small Checks* (1986) and *Large Checks* (1999) cropped chessboard grid paintings, allude to the open-ended possibilities of such games at the same time as they make light of the generation of minimalist geometric and grid painters that preceded Levine's in New York.

Over more than four decades, Levine has played out an ambitious "art-making game" with the goal of introducing the entirety of modernist art and modernist-adapted ethnographic imagery into the purview of postmodernist subject matter. In her work, new insights are arrived at by reexamining, re-framing, and recombining past images in new contexts and applied to new ends.

Unlike many other artworks, which envelop the viewer solely in the present moment, Levine's works place the viewer in two or more timeframes at once: the era and milieu of the work referred to as well as the moment in which the viewer has his or her own unique encounter.

Levine's work, with its wide variety of subjects and media but with its repetition of images and grouped formats, which she refers to as "posses," is evidence that she is admittedly a "reluctant moralist, [who] make[s] art that suggests a simultaneous longing for [both] anarchy and order."[15]

Like Zen koans, her works first appear as deceptively simple gestures that then lead us to profound realizations. Like the air we breathe, her ideas are light and fresh, and utterly essential.

NOTES

1 *Pictures*, organized by Douglas Crimp, was on view at Artists Space, 105 Hudson Street, New York City, September 24–October 29, 1977, and also included the work of Troy Brauntuch, Jack Goldstein, Robert Longo, and Philip Smith.

2 Hugo Ball, *Flight Out of Time: A Dada Diary*, ed. John Elderfield, trans. Ann Raimes (Berkeley: University of California Press, 1996), p. 34. First published 1927 in German.

3 Jack Damer, letter to the author, March 18, 2015. Damer was Levine's lithography professor at the University of Wisconsin–Madison.

4 Jeanne Siegel, interview with Sherrie Levine, "After Sherrie Levine," *Arts Magazine* (June/Summer 1985), p. 246. See p. 36 in this volume.

5 Siegel, "After Sherrie Levine," p. 255. See p. 45 in this volume.

6 Jeanne Siegel, "The Anxiety of Influence, Head On: A Conversation with Sherrie Levine," in *Sherrie Levine*. Exh. cat. (Zurich: Kunsthalle Zürich, 1991), p. 18.

7 Douglas Crimp, "The Photographic Activity of Postmodernism," *October* 15 (Winter 1980), p. 99.

8 *The Probert Encyclopaedia of Mythology*, accessed at cakravartin.com. See also "The Classic Domino," *Historical Fancy Dress* (blog), August 2, 2011, https://www.historicalfancydress.com/2011/08/the-classic-domino.html, which offers descriptions from Ardern Holt, *Fancy Dresses Described*, 6th ed. (London: Debenham & Freebody, 1896) and *Masquerades, Tableaux and Drills* (New York: The Butterick Publishing Company, 1906).

9 Siegel, "The Anxiety of Influence," p. 17.

10 Rodney P. Carlisle, ed., *Encyclopedia of Play in Today's Society* (Los Angeles: Sage, 2009), pp. 181–182; Andrew Lo, "China's Passion for Pai: Playing Cards, Dominoes, and Mahjong," in *Asian Games: The Art of Contest*, ed. Colin Mackenzie and Irving Finkel (New York: Asia Society, 2004), pp. 222–224.

11 William Newton, *Newton's London Journal of Arts and Sciences* 23 (London, 1866), p. 334. The Jacquard machine is a device fitted to a Jacquard loom that simplifies the process of manufacturing textiles with complex patterns.

12 Lo, "China's Passion for Pai," p. 223.

13 Lo, "China's Passion for Pai," p. 223.

14 Lo, "China's Passion for Pai," p. 224.

15 Sherrie Levine, quoted in Hunter Drohojowska, "Stop Making Sense," *ARTnews* (October 1989), p. 151.

After Sherrie Levine
Jeanne Siegel

The following interview was originally published in the June/ Summer 1985 issue of Arts Magazine, *New York.*

A Promethean thief or an immoralist confiscator, Sherrie Levine challenges art at its matrix of model and originality.

For the past eight years Sherrie Levine has dealt with appropriated imagery. Her first confiscations were collages. She cut pictures out of books and magazines and glued them onto mats. Since then she has made copies of photographs after Eliot Porter, Edward Weston, Walker Evans, and Alexander Rodchenko; drawings after Willem de Kooning, Egon Schiele, and Kasimir Malevich; watercolors after Mondrian, Matisse, El Lissitzky, and Léger, to name a few.

After the initial shock of discovering the artist's audacity in quoting and mounting famous artists' works, the question becomes: what then? Does her magnetism rest merely in the paradox of originality through copies? Does she recast the principle of the copy in a new and contemporary light? Why does she choose only male artists to copy? How does she view her own work and the considerable rhetoric that has gathered around it?

JEANNE SIEGEL You were educated at the University of Wisconsin. How did this influence your direction, if indeed it did at all?

SHERRIE LEVINE I think growing up in the Midwest certainly did. I grew up in St. Louis and I went to school in Wisconsin for eight years. I got my undergraduate and graduate degrees there. Having the feeling of somehow being outside of the mainstream of the art world had a lot to do with my feelings about art. Seeing everything through magazines and books—I got a lot of my sense of what art looked like in terms of surface and finish.

JS One feature that serves as a clue is the way you preserve in the copy the faint tints or discolorations that were the result of the photo-printing or reproductive process. This distinguishes it from the original. So you were conscious of the notion of a secondary source from the start.

SL Yes. It was the sixties. I was in college and a minimal painter and minimal art looked even flatter in magazines. I felt that my work was becoming very mannerist and empty for me. I began to use photography as a way of introducing representational imagery into my work.

JS It seems significant that you received your graduate degree in photo-printmaking.

SL I was interested in the idea of multiple images and mechanical reproduction. I did a lot of commercial art for money from the time I was in college until very recently.

JS Do you see that as an influence also?

SL I think it had a lot to do with it. I was really interested in how they dealt with the idea of originality. If they wanted an image, they'd just take it. It was never an issue of morality; it was always an issue of utility. There was no sense that images belonged to anybody; all images were in the public domain and as an artist I found that very liberating.

JS There are specific methods that commercial artists use, for example, tracing.

SL And the use of copy cameras.

JS It occurred to me that your process of working from prints is somewhat like the custom popular in the seventeenth century of copying a painting to make a print. What the print artist did was to remain true to the composition and poses of the figures, but they didn't necessarily hold to the original expression on people's faces. They thought of the print as being slightly original. In other words, it stepped away to become something new.

SL I think that copies and prints were the main way of distributing images at that time, before photography.

JS The Caravaggio exhibition currently at the Metropolitan Museum focuses the idea of copying in another way. An original Caravaggio is mounted next to a copy or to works that have been attributed to Caravaggio. The exhibition reflects the modern need for uniqueness, whereas at that time one commissioned a copy of a master because one loved the painting or because a pious patron might want an image of John the Baptist.

SL So much of our sense of art history is based on copies, fakes, and forgeries. I just read *The Caravaggio Conspiracy*, a book about art theft and forgery written by an investigative reporter. While he's looking for a stolen Caravaggio painting, he comes across an incredible amount of forged art. There's always been a lot of it around. Some entire museum collections are forgeries.

JS My point is that in the sixteenth century a copy was not necessarily frowned upon. People respected copies.

SL I think it was a different relationship to history at that time. It was more like an Oriental belief in tradition. You strove to be fully mature in your tradition. Originality was not an issue. I think that's where modernism was a real break.

JS In the process of copying from an original painting to make a print, the size is reduced. This seems to have some connection to your work.

SL In most cases it is reduced from the original but maintains the size of the bookplate. Maintaining a uniform format has a democratizing effect on the images that I like. The watercolors and drawings are traced out of books onto eleven-by-fourteen-inch pieces of paper. The paintings are easel-size on twenty-by-twenty-four-inch boards.

The pictures I make are really ghosts of ghosts; their relationship to the original images is tertiary, i.e., three or four times removed. By the time a picture becomes a bookplate it's already been rephotographed several times. When I started doing this work, I wanted to make a picture which contradicted itself. I wanted to put a picture on top of a picture so that there are times when both pictures disappear and other times when they're both manifest; that vibration is basically what the work's about for me—that space in the middle where there's no picture.

JS Can you elaborate on what originality means to you?

SL It's not that I don't think that the word "originality" means anything or has no meaning. I just think it's gotten a very narrow meaning lately. What I think about in terms of my work is broadening the definitions of the word "original." I think of originality as a trope. There is no such thing as an ahistorical activity (I mean history in terms of one's personal history, too).

JS What about the idea behind the introduction of your hand? This came about when you stopped copying photographs and began to draw "de Koonings."

SL A lot of the most sophisticated psychoanalytic and feminist critiques about art and film posit the supremacy of the visual over all our other senses in a patriarchal society. I think a lot of what's alienating and oppressive about our media culture is its voyeuristic aspect. It's ironic that most of this theory that is applied to art has been mainly in support of photographic work. There seems to be a denial of the rest of the body. In art, the hand becomes the metonymical symbol for the body.

JS There is something in the work that suggests that you thoroughly enjoy this hand work. It's visceral on occasion.

SL Oh yes. There's no other reason to do it. For me, art's basically about pleasure. I'm not saying there's no pleasure in making or looking at photography, but there are definitely some different kinds of pleasure in making and looking at painting.

JS Can you see this process of copying from a print as a manifestation of the recent revival of craft?

SL I wouldn't want to deny that. I think a lot of people see this evidence of the body as antidotal to an overmechanized culture.

JS Do you concentrate on matching? Do you investigate and reconstruct the original colors?

SL I give it a couple of shots if necessary. I stop when the color works with what I've already got on my page. I don't make it a photo-realist activity because that's mechanistic again and then I'm back where I started. I'm trying not to be tyrannized by the original image. What I'm really interested in is constructing my relationship to the image.

JS Does your choice of artist or particular work of that artist have any relation to this question of craft?

SL Painting very complex images would become drudgery for me, and I have no interest in that.

JS In titling your works *After Kasimir Malevich* or *After Egon Schiele* you are alluding to an accepted earlier convention in art—one which flowered in the baroque period and continued into the nineteenth century. Viewed historically, you could say that during the Renaissance Vasari established a canon of greatness which was adhered to by later generations. Is there a parallel to this pattern in that you chose the so-called heroes from earlier modernism?

SL There is. I think about it a lot in psychological terms. I mean, in an Oedipal way, about the authority of the father and the authority of the father's desire. My work is so much about desire and its triangular nature. Desire is always mediated through someone else's desire.

JS And this is why the someone else that you appropriate is always male?

SL A lot of what my work has been about since the beginning has been realizing the difficulties of situating myself in the art world as a woman, because the art world is so much an arena for the celebration of male desire.

JS So his desire becomes yours in order to make this explicit? Then it's in the nature of a critique, really.

SL I prefer the word "analysis." Somebody recently referred to my watercolors as position papers. One thing I'd like to make clear is that I make the things I want to make. The language and the rhetoric come afterward when I attempt to describe to myself and to other people what I've done, but I'm not making the art to make a point or to illustrate a theory. I'm making the picture I want to look at which is what I think everybody does. The desire comes first.

JS Egon Schiele could be considered a possible exception to your choices of "greats." How did that come about?

SL I haven't done this just in relationship to the history books, although obviously they form everybody's ideas about what's important. It's also been about my own personal relationship to this work, and Schiele is somebody who's been important to me.

JS Why?

SL There is something in his eroticism that strikes a chord. Partly it's the self-conscious representation of his own narcissism. I don't want to say too much on this topic. A girl's gotta keep some secrets.

JS There seems to exist a kind of contradiction. Does your attitude have something in common with Lichtenstein's? Although he parodied the abstract-expressionist brushstroke, he said he liked it.

SL It's a dialectical relationship, I think, which is the kind of relationship one has to authority. That's where the irony in the work is located. But the parody is not in relationship to the original; it's in how I perceive the original.

JS In discussing the history of the changing approach to the object in the twentieth century, particularly in relation to its uniqueness and originality, Suzi Gablik (*Has Modernism Failed?*) mentions your duplications of photographs of famous photographers. This follows a discussion of Rauschenberg's *Erased Drawing of de Kooning's*. It seemed to me that in a way you are doing the reverse of what Rauschenberg did: whereas he wipes out, you are putting it back, albeit in another form.

SL A lot of people do see my work as an erasure. I think the people it offends most imagine it's an erasure.

JS In what sense?

SL In the sense that it's a screen memory—a memory that blocks a more primal memory.

JS What was your reaction to Gablik's analysis of your intentions and her conclusions? I quote:
> Levine lays no claim to traditional notions of "creativity." By willfully refusing to acknowledge any difference between the originals and her own reproductions, she is addressing her work in a subversive way to the current mass cult for collecting photographs, and their absorption

into the art market as one more expensive commodity. Obviously ideas like these are successful as a negation of commodity-oriented culture. Only until commodity culture succeeds in accommodating even these "pirated" creations and turning them into yet another saleable item within the framework of institutionalized art-world distribution . . . at which point they become more parasitic than critical, feeding on the very system they are meant to criticize.

SL My works were never intended to be anything but commodities. It's taken a while for the work to sell but it has always been my hope that it would, and that it would wind up in collections and in museums. You know, money talks but it don't sing.

The work is always in a dialectical relationship to the notion of originality. Originality was always something I was thinking about, but there's also the idea of ownership and property. Lawrence Weiner has this nice quote about wanting to make art that makes us think about our relationship to the material world. That's something that I feel very close to. It's not that I'm trying to deny that people own things. That isn't even the point. The point is that people *want* to own things, which is more interesting to me. What does it mean to own something, and, stranger still, what does it mean to own an image?

JS Do you believe that viewers outside of the inner circle of the art world know what it is?

SL There's a lot of irony in this problem because when I first started making this work I thought that anybody could understand it. It didn't seem elitist to me at all. Any thoughtful person could understand that a picture of a picture was a strange object. I still think it's true that anybody can understand the work. Some people think they're not understanding it, that there's something that they don't know about, and that's when they feel deceived or betrayed. A picture of a picture is a strange thing and it brings up lots of contradictions; it seems to me that anybody can understand that. Obviously not everybody likes it.

JS Some of the people who look at it might not even know the original, so they don't have a basis of comparison.

SL I don't mind that. People enjoy or don't enjoy the pictures that I make. My pictures have other relationships than their relationship to me. I like to think that it's complex work and it can be appreciated on a lot of levels, or not appreciated on a lot of levels. For one thing, I think this work is very funny. I'm always surprised when people apologize to me for thinking it's funny. I want the work to be funny, but that doesn't mean I'm not serious.

JS The practice of copying another existing artwork is often identified with the formative years of an artist. Are you connected to that or is it just coincidental?

SL No; I've thought about it a lot, especially when I think of what I want to do next. I realize that this was something that I needed to do. It's interesting to me because I never consciously thought of myself as a student or apprentice, but I realize that it's a step that I wanted to take. I'm not in any way demeaning the work or saying that it's immature. But the irony to me is that people were so worried about what I would do next and it's been so generative for me.

JS Could you discuss some of those developments generated by the use of the copy? For example, in the *1917* show (Nature Morte Gallery, October 1984), you coupled works by two artists that gave them a meaning beyond their showing separately.

SL My appropriated images have been dealing with the modernists and their ideas, a lot of which were utopian. This summer when I was doing drawings by both Malevich and Schiele, I started to realize that the dates all circulated around 1917. It was amazing to me that these two extremely radical and yet seemingly mutually exclusive activities could be going on at the same time. I thought it might make sense to show Schiele's erotic drawings with Malevich's suprematist works.

JS So this represented a comment on your part on the naive optimism in art's capacity to change political systems?

SL When I began this work I was thinking about my relationship to the utopian ideas expressed by the modernists. We no longer have the naive optimism in art's capacity to change political systems—an aspiration that many modernist projects shared.

As postmodernists we find that simple faith very moving,
but our relationship to that simplicity is necessarily complex.

JS In the more recent *Repetitions* show (Hunter College Art
Gallery, March 1985), you used another strategy. You repeated
six pencil drawings of an identical composition by Malevich.

SL When Maurice Berger, the curator, told me he was doing a
show called *Repetitions* and wanted me to be in it, I was very
excited because I had been thinking about doing a piece where
an image was repeated several times. Repetition's implied in
the work anyway (i.e., if you can make one copy, then you can
make any number of them). So I thought this was a perfect
opportunity to repeat an image six times.

JS Also, you now seem to be anxious to keep works together
in a group that previously you showed singly. This is true of the
works in the current Whitney Biennial.

SL People have been loath to discuss the work iconographically for some reason. Last month I was talking to the writer
Howard Singerman who lives in Los Angeles; he was saying
that people tend to look at the work as if it starts at the frame
and goes out, as opposed to looking at the picture from the
frame in. What he meant was that we've become so sensitized
to context that we sometimes just see the picture as a hole
in the wall. In fact, they are pictures. They're very complicated
pictures, but they can be read iconographically. The images
in the *1917* show are crosses and people masturbating. Most
people who have written about the work have either ignored
or denied the iconographic content.

I think a lot of people seem to get lost in the gap and think
that there's no picture there, when in fact there are two
pictures there.

JS Coming back to appropriation again, how do you feel that
you differ, for example, from Andy Warhol, to whom you have
expressed an affinity?

SL There's an emptiness in Warhol's work that's always been
very interesting to me because of that vibration I was talking
about. There are three spaces: the original image, his image,
and then a space in between, a sort of Zen emptiness—an
oblivion in his work that's always been very interesting to me.

JS Your choices of images are quite different from his.

SL Yes, although I often think that Warhol chooses images that he loves, which is what makes the work much less nasty than it might be, and that's important to me, too.

JS A few months ago you were invited to show in an exhibition, *Production Re: Production*, which dealt explicitly with appropriation and you refused to participate. Why?

SL I never aspired to belong to a school of appropriators. "Appropriation" is a label that makes me cringe because it's come to signify a polemic; as an artist, I don't like to think of myself as a polemicist.

I think I've softened a lot since I first started talking about this work. I should make it clear that I don't think art should be any one thing—my work only has meaning in relationship to everyone else's project. It has no meaning in isolation, and on the level of desire everyone's project is different. I believe that one of the most important advances that feminist artists and writers have made has been in establishing the possibility of difference, the possibility of a plurality of voices and gazes. It's important to me that my work be situated in the totality of contemporary art-making. I'm not trying to supplant anything; my work is in addition. The idea is to broaden the discussion, not to narrow it.

JS In the process of becoming recognized, you have been grouped with certain artists referred to as "deconstructors." In what ways do you separate yourself from them?

SL I may have a more traditional relationship to art. I grew up in St. Louis which has a very beautiful museum that I loved going to as a child. Although I have a conflicted relationship to art world institutions and culture industries, I do love art and modernist art in particular.

JS Your work has triggered a good deal of rhetoric. I am interested in your response to some of the ideas that have been articulated. One, which we have already touched on briefly, is the role of the Oedipus complex as stated by Lacan. In an article on Lacan and Freud (*The Massachusetts Review*, Summer 1979), Neal H. Bruss says:

For Lacan, it is the resolution of the Oedipus complex which reduces the infinitude of potential desires and linguistic choices to a manageable system; it does so by initiating the child into a third order, the "Symbolic," the code of language and custom by which the larger community operates. Lacan takes the Oedipal resolution as a parable like the mirror stage, justified by Freud's own recognition that it could be reached without the child having actually witnessed a primal scene. Lacan's parablistic reading of the Oedipal complex, for example, does not exclude female children from the Oedipal role. . . .

SL That's why I've been so interested in critiques of Freud and Lacan by feminists like Jacqueline Rose and Juliet Mitchell, because they show us a way to have ideas about feminine desire. They talk about how culture creates an indivisible bond between gender and sexuality, a bond which becomes a yoke, a bond which is even more complex in the case of femininity.

JS You have expressed interest in Jean Baudrillard's critiques. According to Craig Owens (*Art & Social Change, U.S.A.*, April 1983), Baudrillard argued that power is no longer exercised exclusively or even primarily through control of the means of production, but through control of the means of representation: the code. What was needed, then, was a critique of representation, but one free from a productivist bias. Owens concludes, "It was such a critique that this new group of artists set out to provide." As you were included in this group, please comment.

SL This writing exposed the indignity of speaking for others. Like most women, I'd gotten pretty tired of being depicted and represented by men.

JS A year ago, when asked whether you anticipated a change in your work away from working "after" other artists, you responded by saying that this was really your desire at the moment. "I'm making the pictures I want to look at," you said, which implied that you were not thinking about any change. How do you feel now?

SL I'm in a transitional period right now. I'm thinking of making more kinds of choices . . . I guess I'm reluctant to speak about it too much yet.

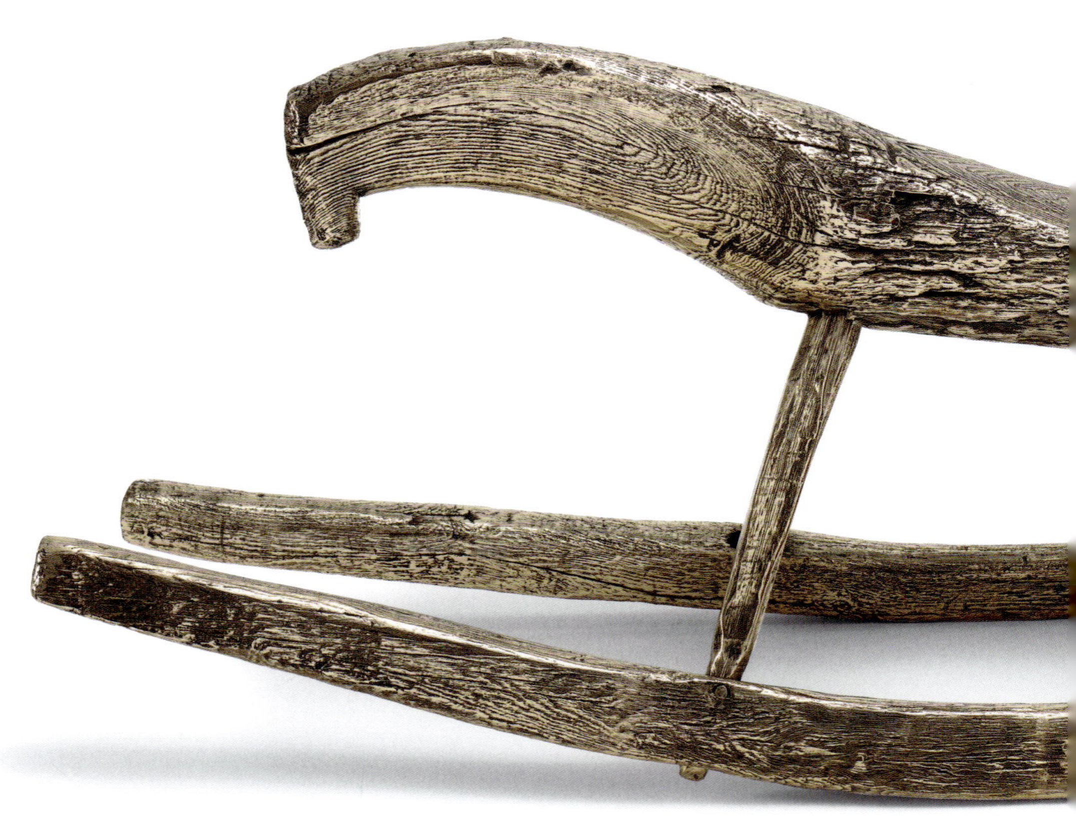

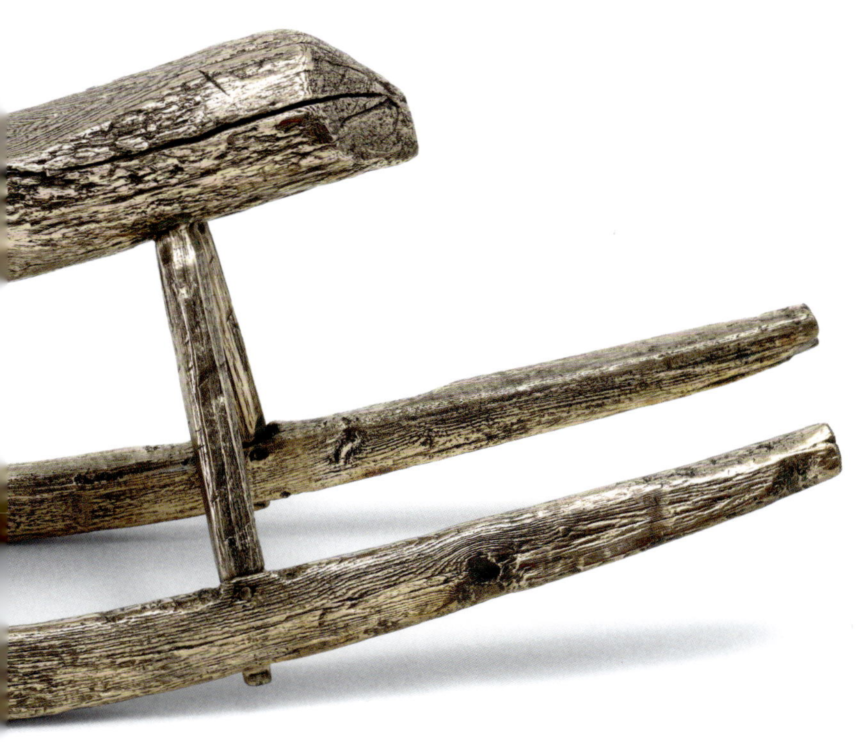

Hobby Horse, 2014
Cast bronze
18 × 55 × 13 inches
45.7 × 139.7 × 33 cm

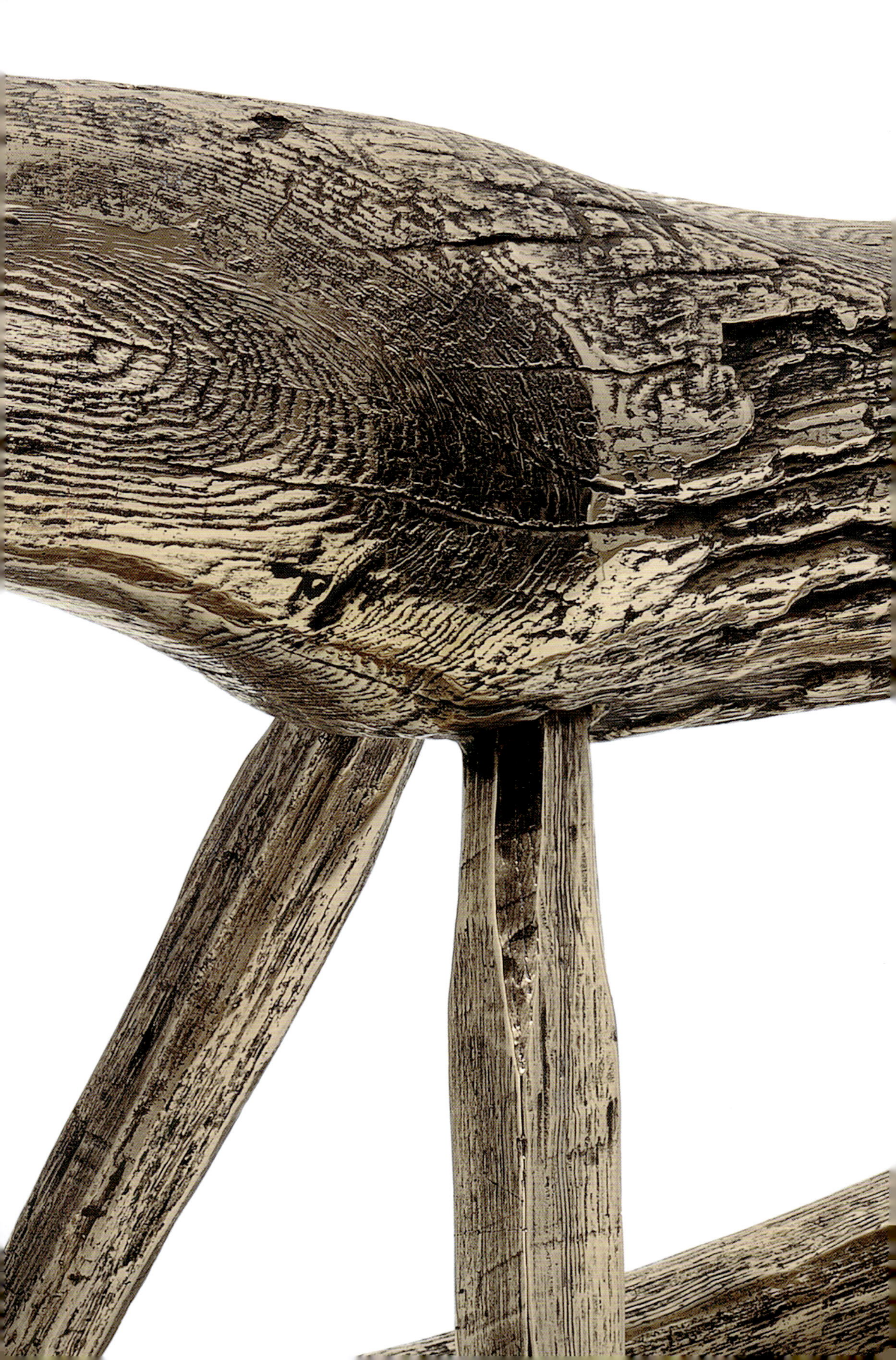

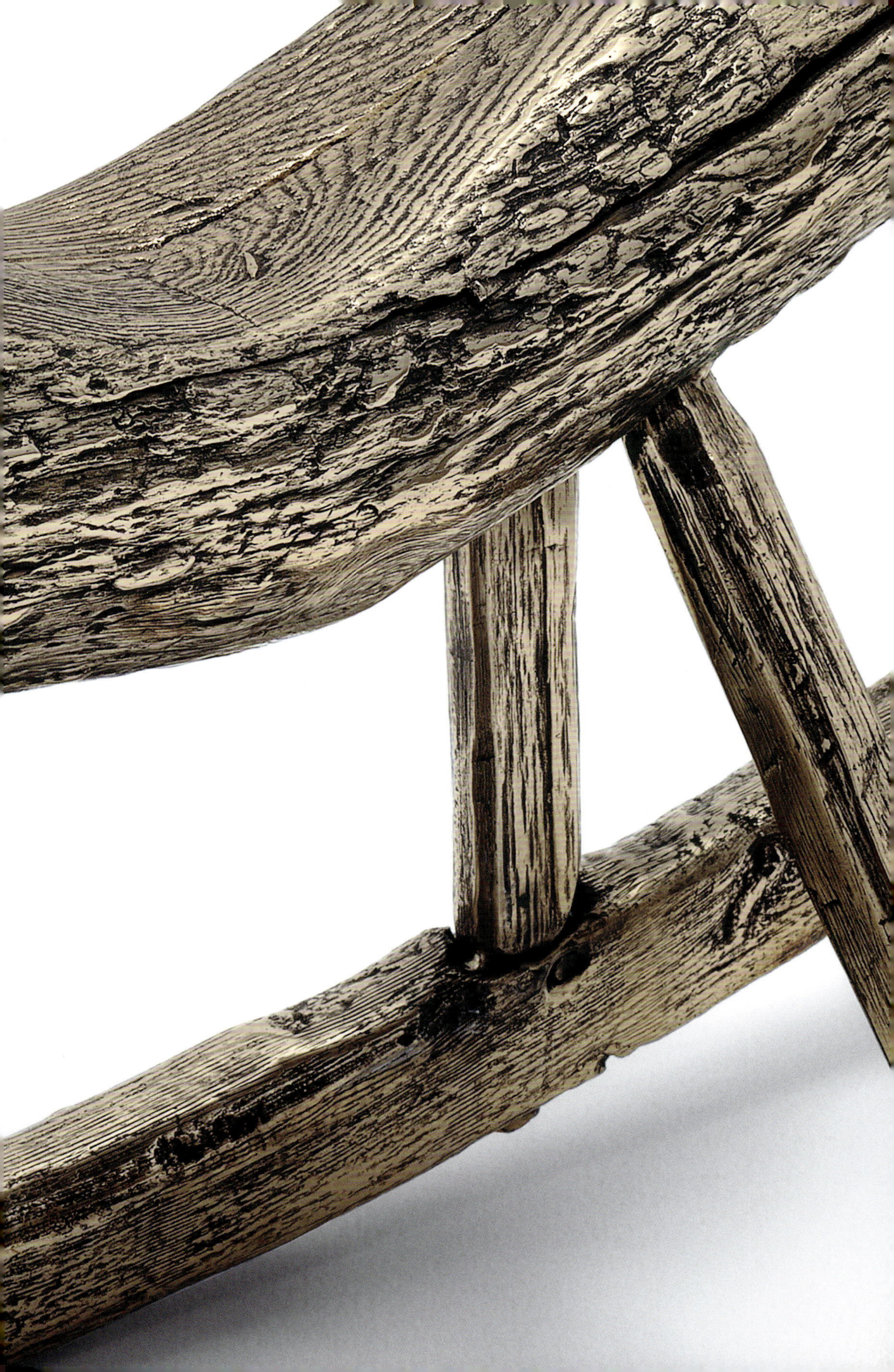

Monochromes After Renoir Nudes

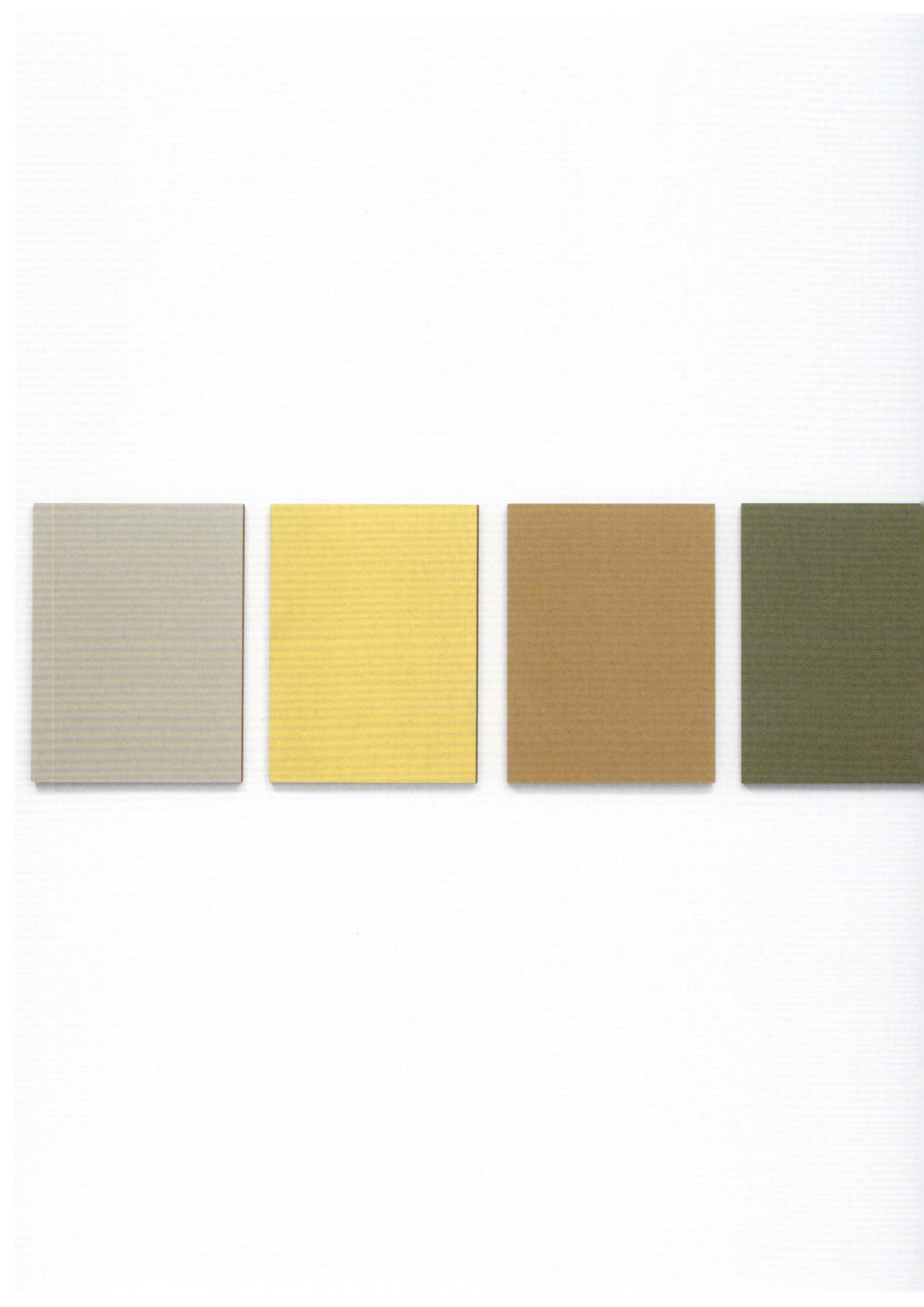

  Installation view, *Monochromes After Renoir Nudes: 1–8*, 2016

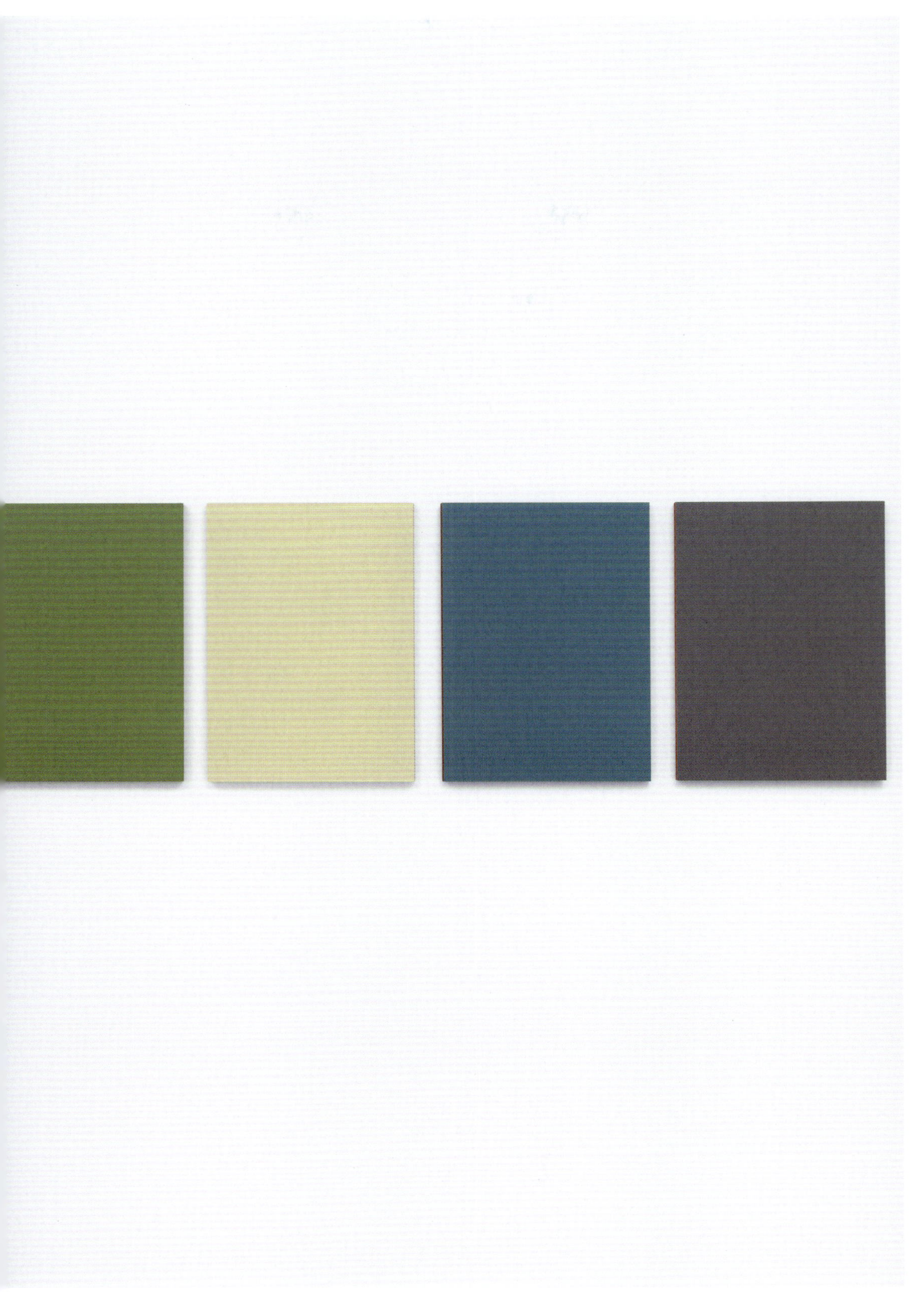

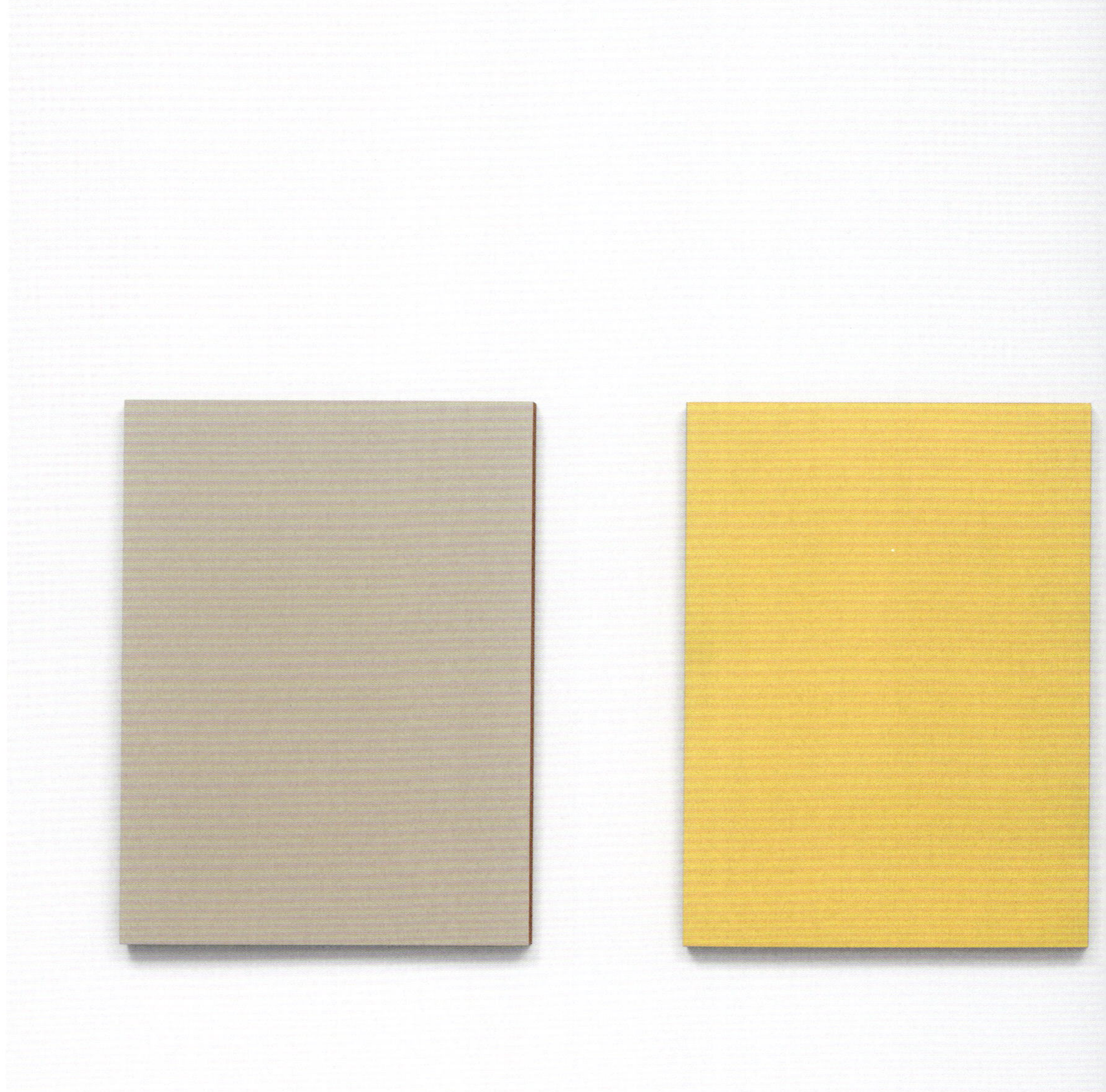

Monochromes After Renoir Nudes: 1–4, 2016
Four oil on mahogany panels
28 × 108 inches
71.1 × 274.3 cm

Monochromes After Renoir Nudes: 5–8, 2016
Four oil on mahogany panels
28 × 108 inches
71.1 × 274.3 cm

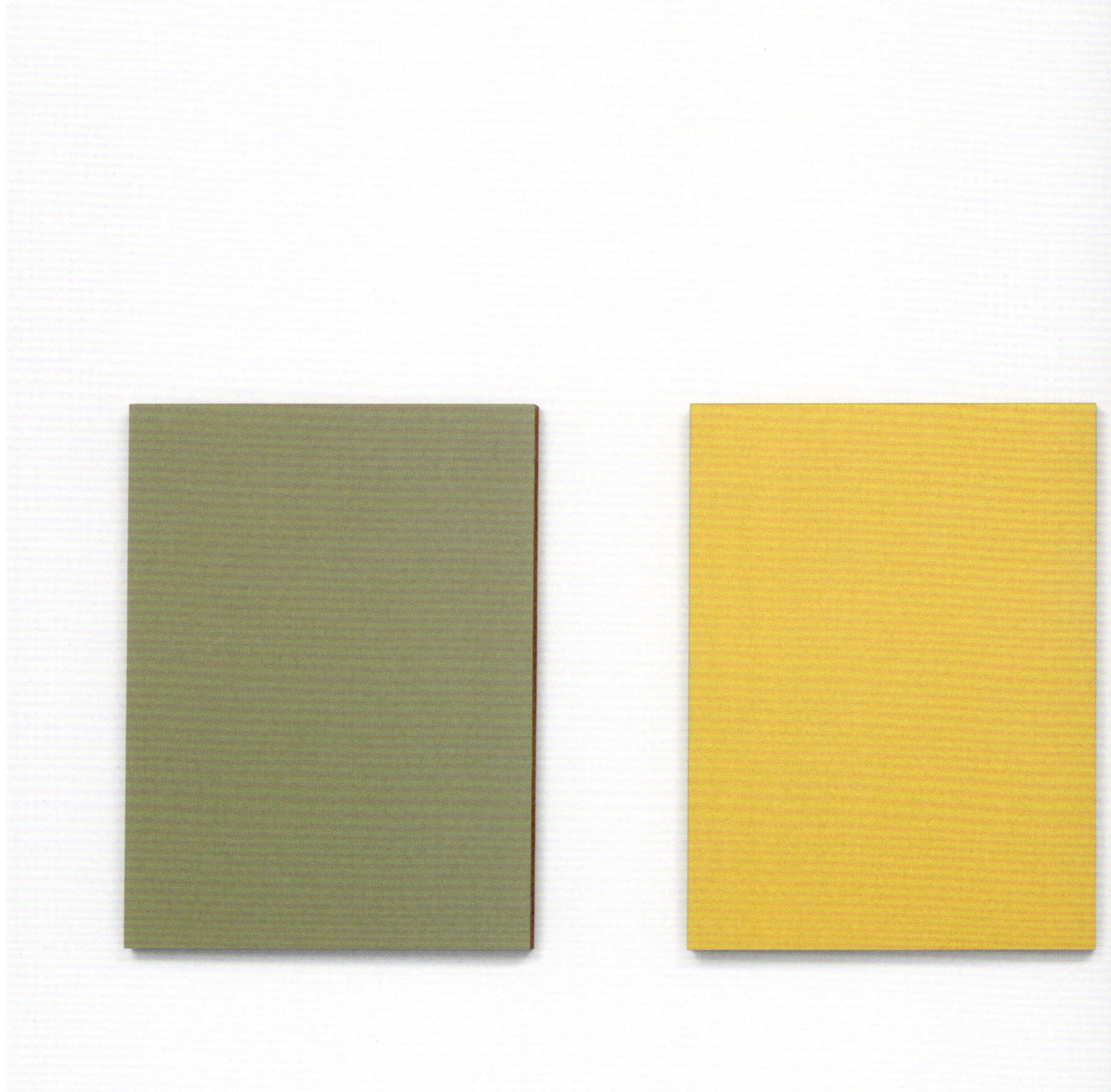

Monochromes After Renoir Nudes: 9–12, 2016
Four oil on mahogany panels
28 × 108 inches
71.1 × 274.3 cm

Monochromes After Renoir Nudes: 13–16, 2016
Four oil on mahogany panels
28 × 108 inches
71.1 × 274.3 cm

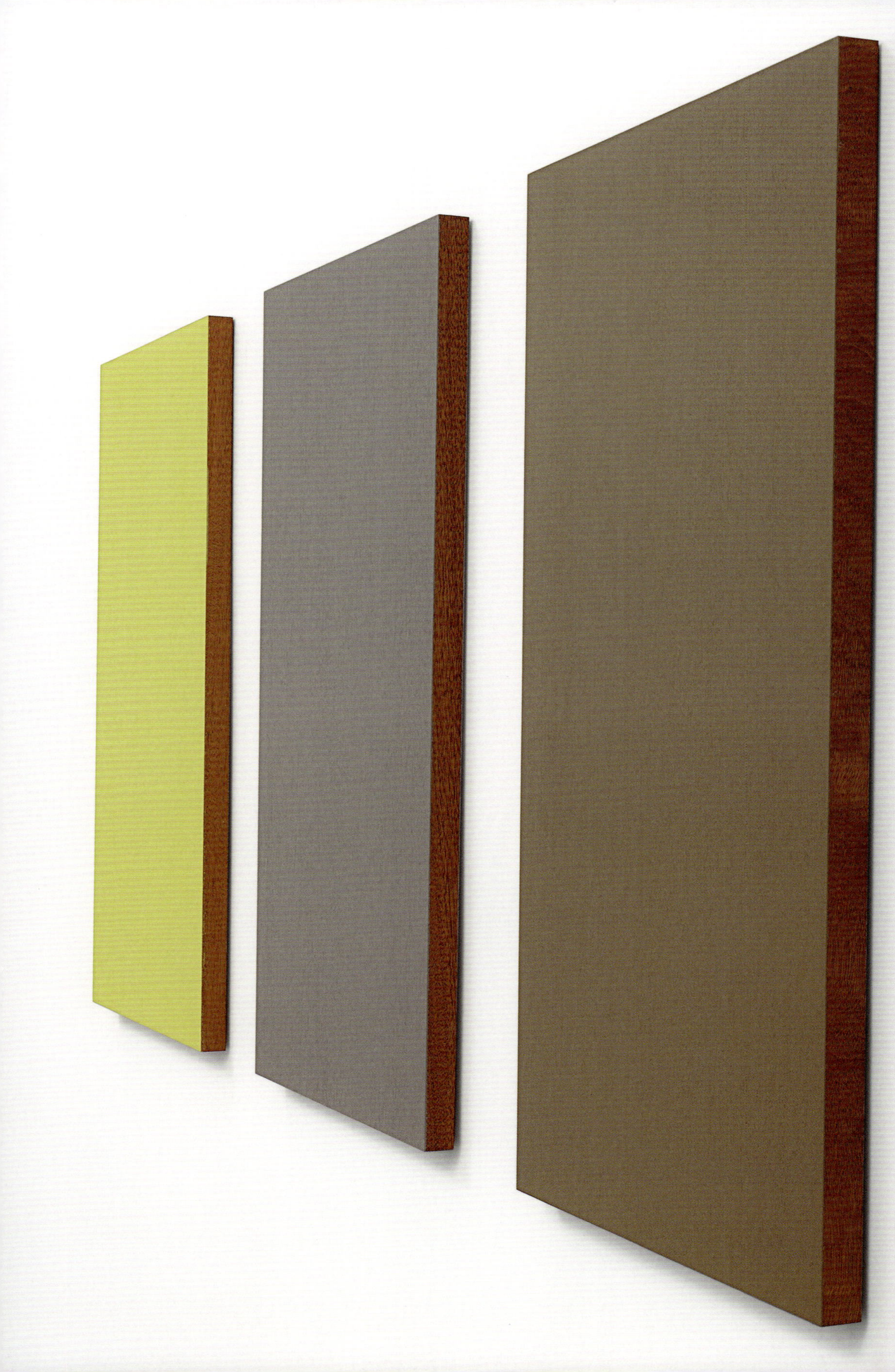

Monochromes After Renoir Nudes: 17–20, 2016
Four oil on mahogany panels
28 × 108 inches
71.1 × 274.3 cm

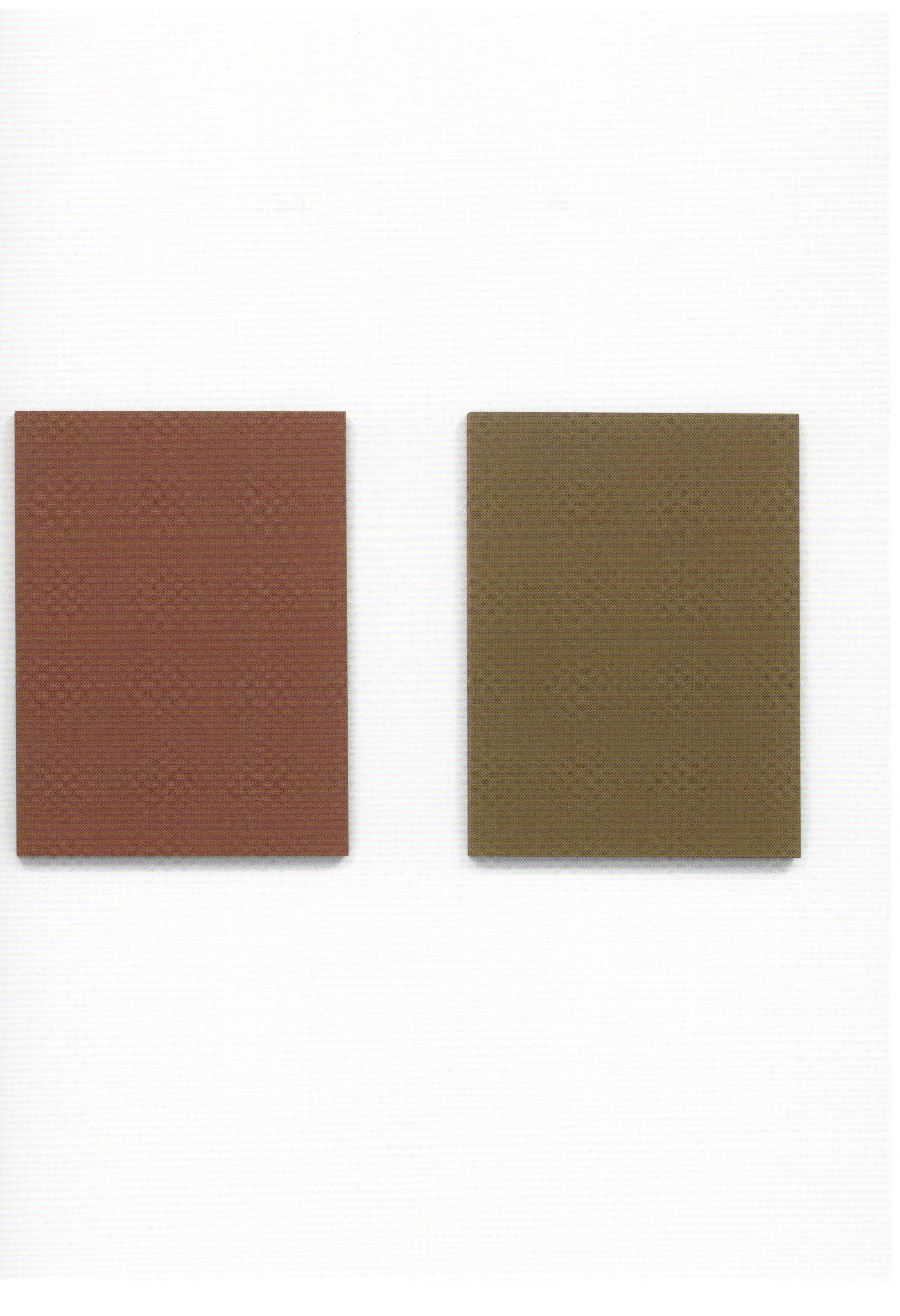

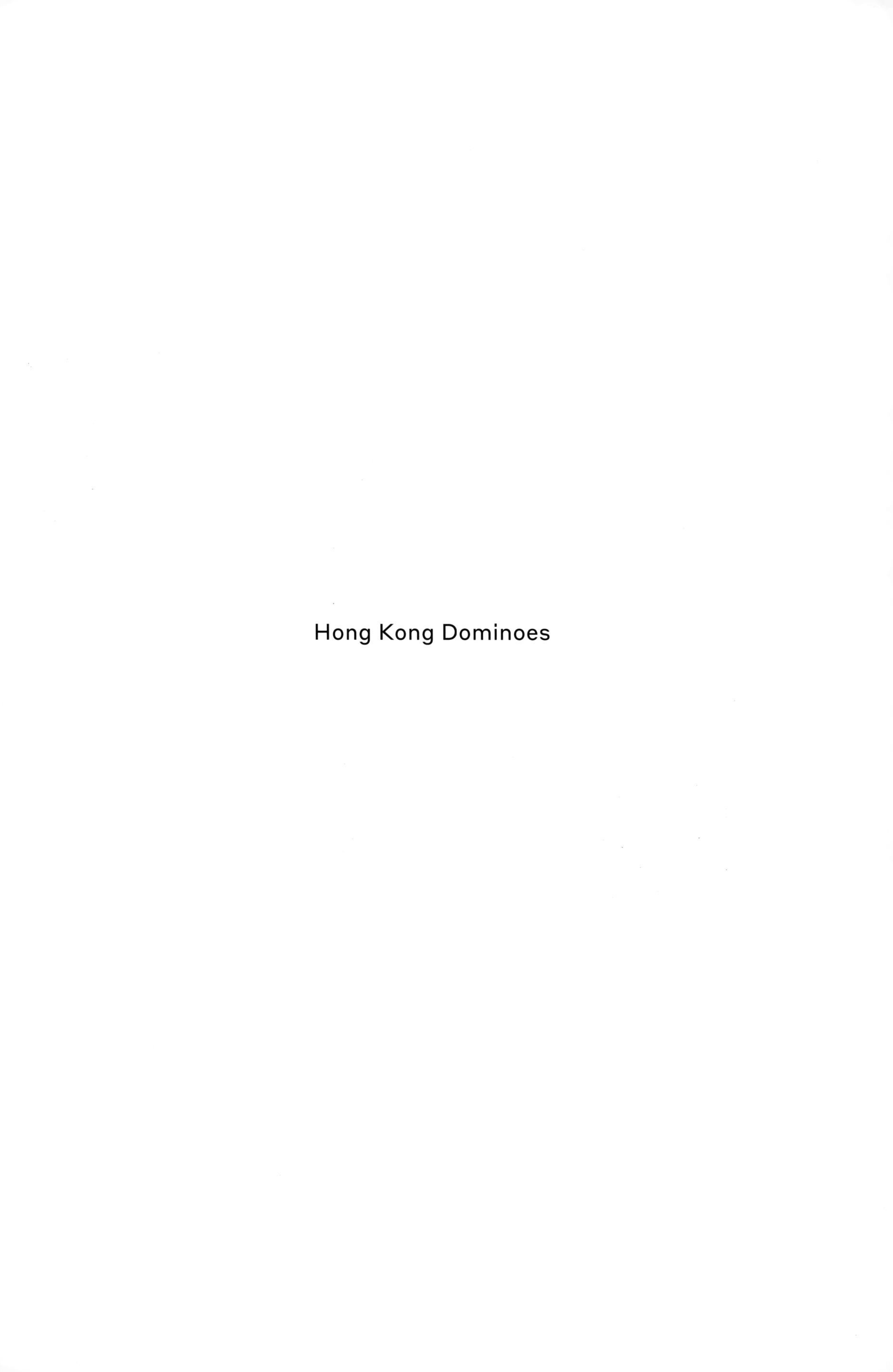

Hong Kong Dominoes

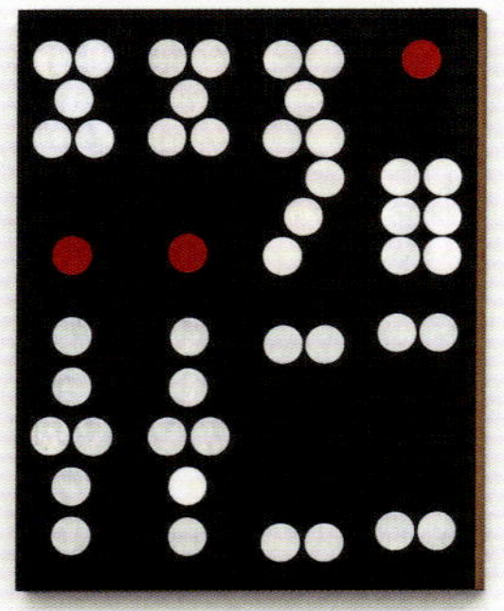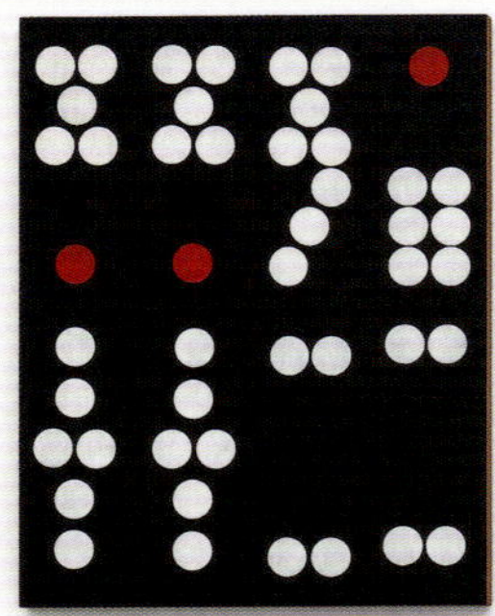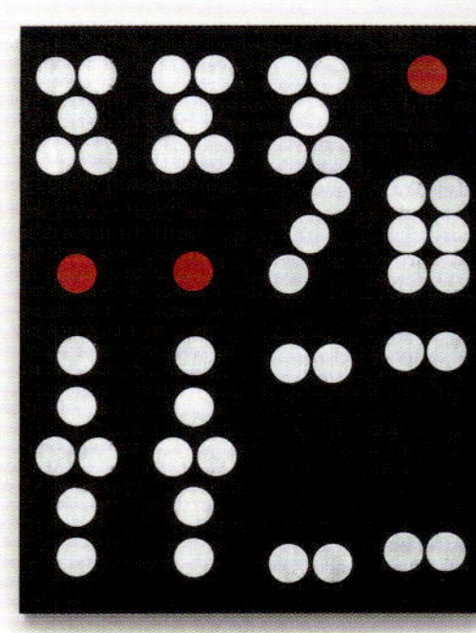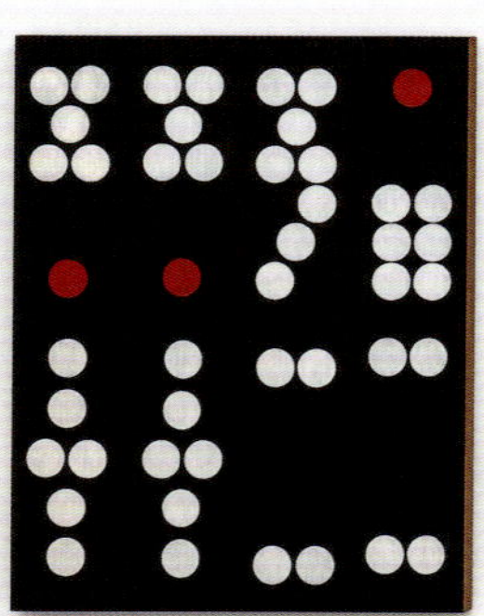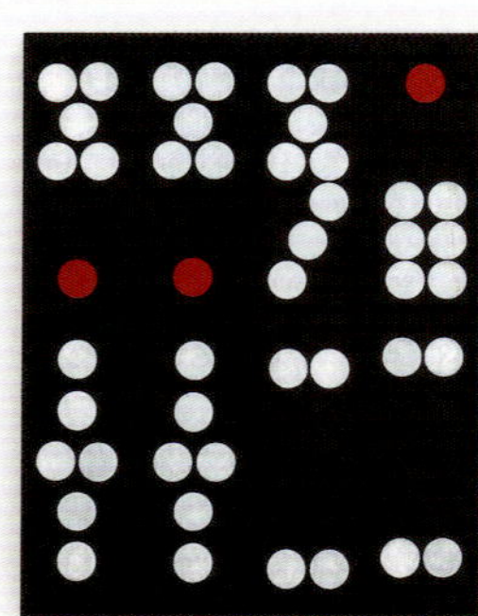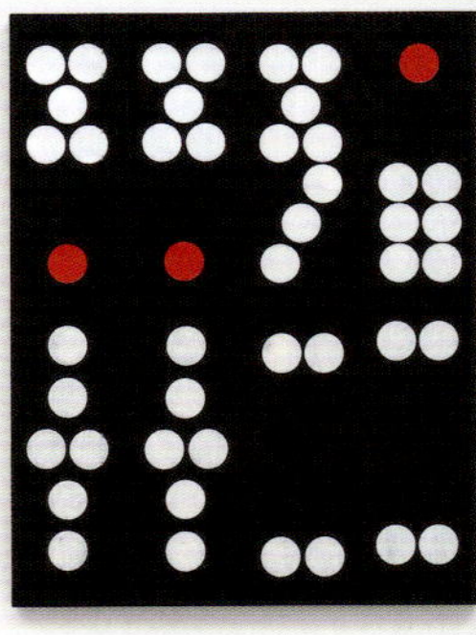

Installation view, *Hong Kong*
Dominoes: 1-12, 2017
Twelve tempera on mahogany panels

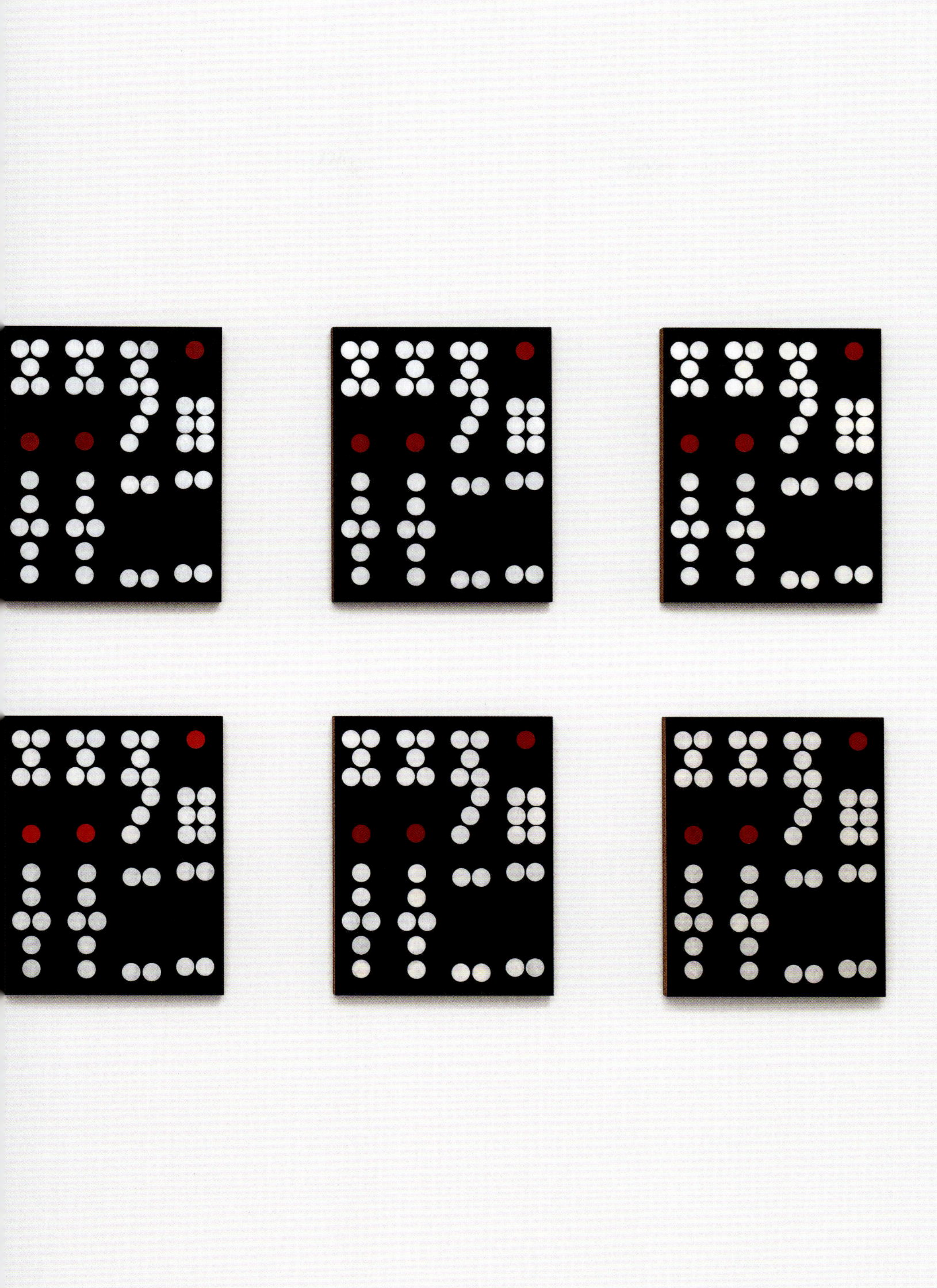

Each: 20 × 16 inches
50.8 × 40.6 cm
Overall dimensions variable

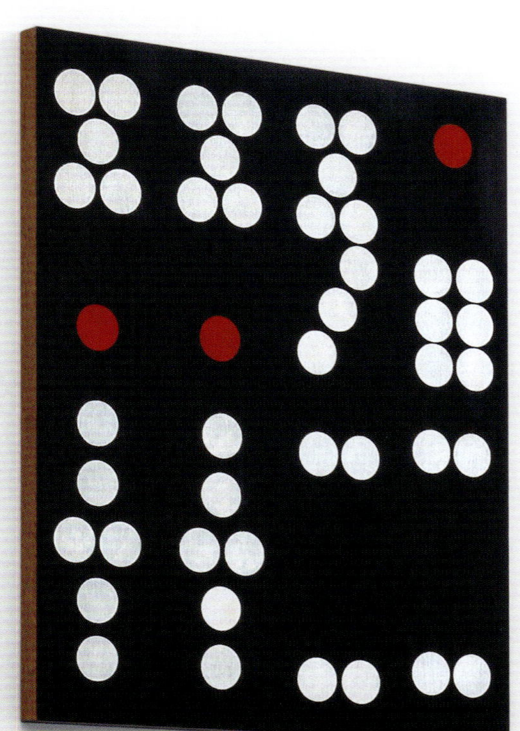
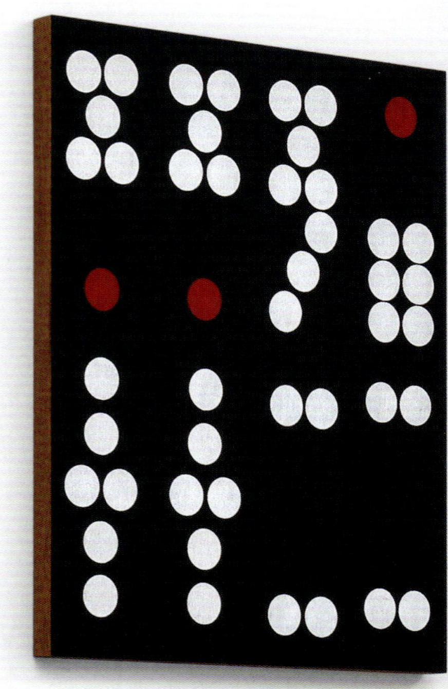
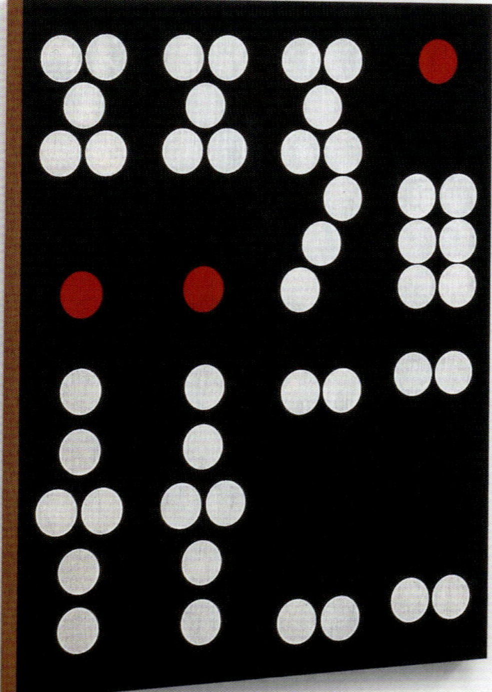
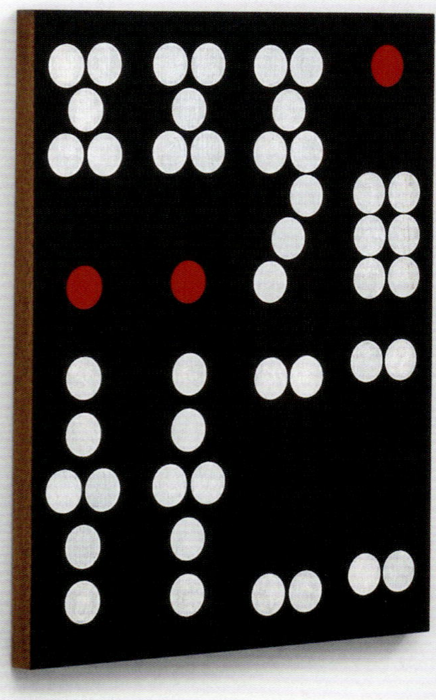

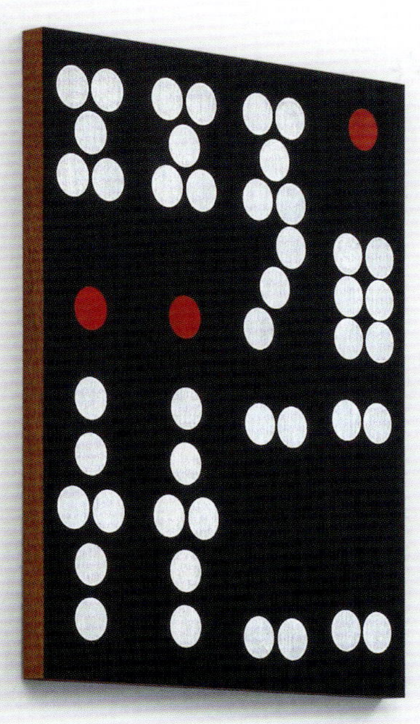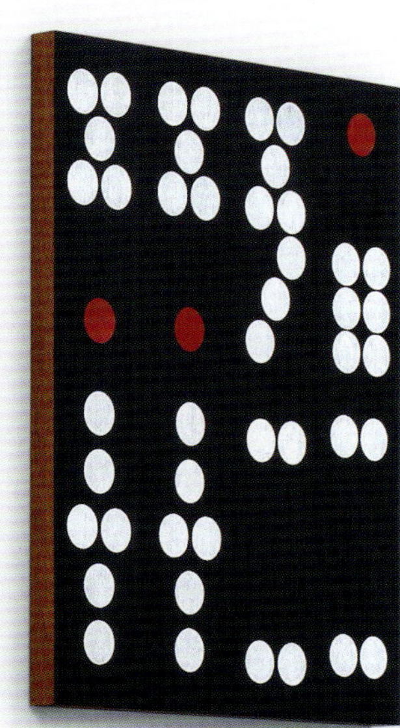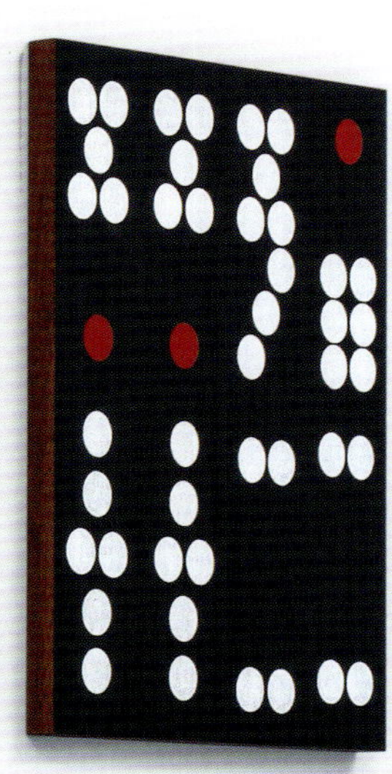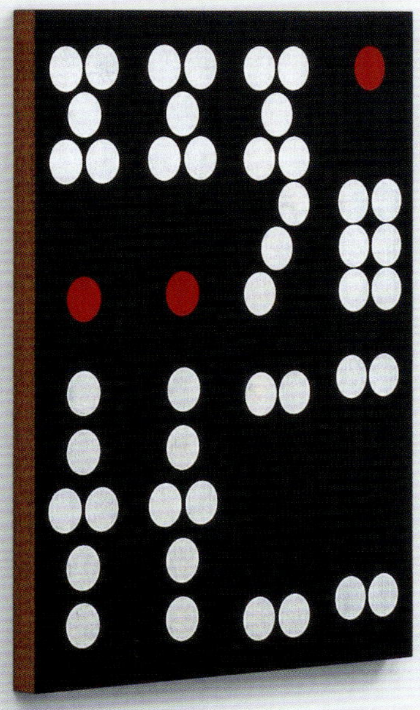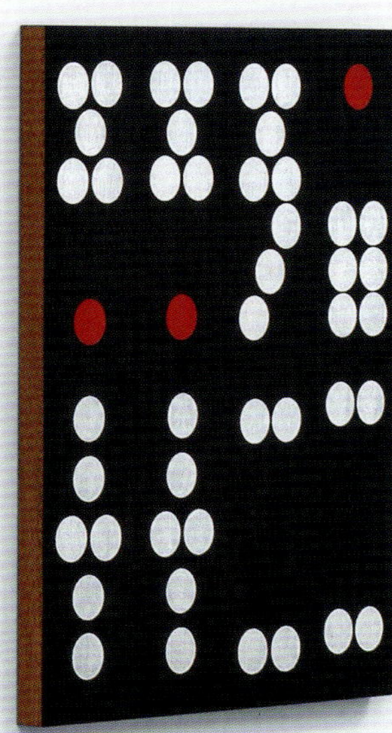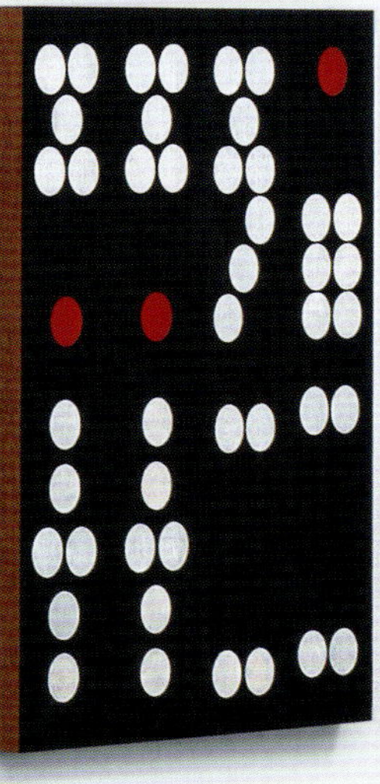

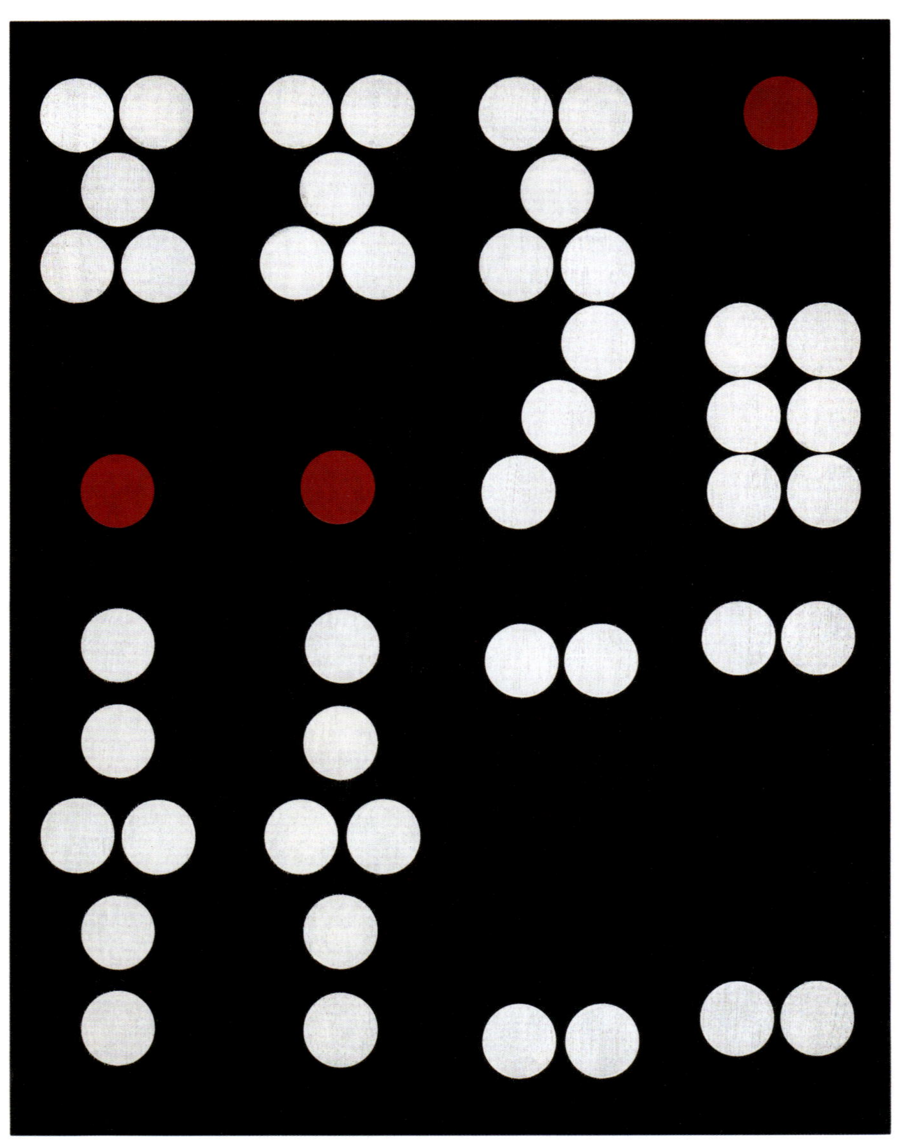

Hong Kong Dominoes: 1

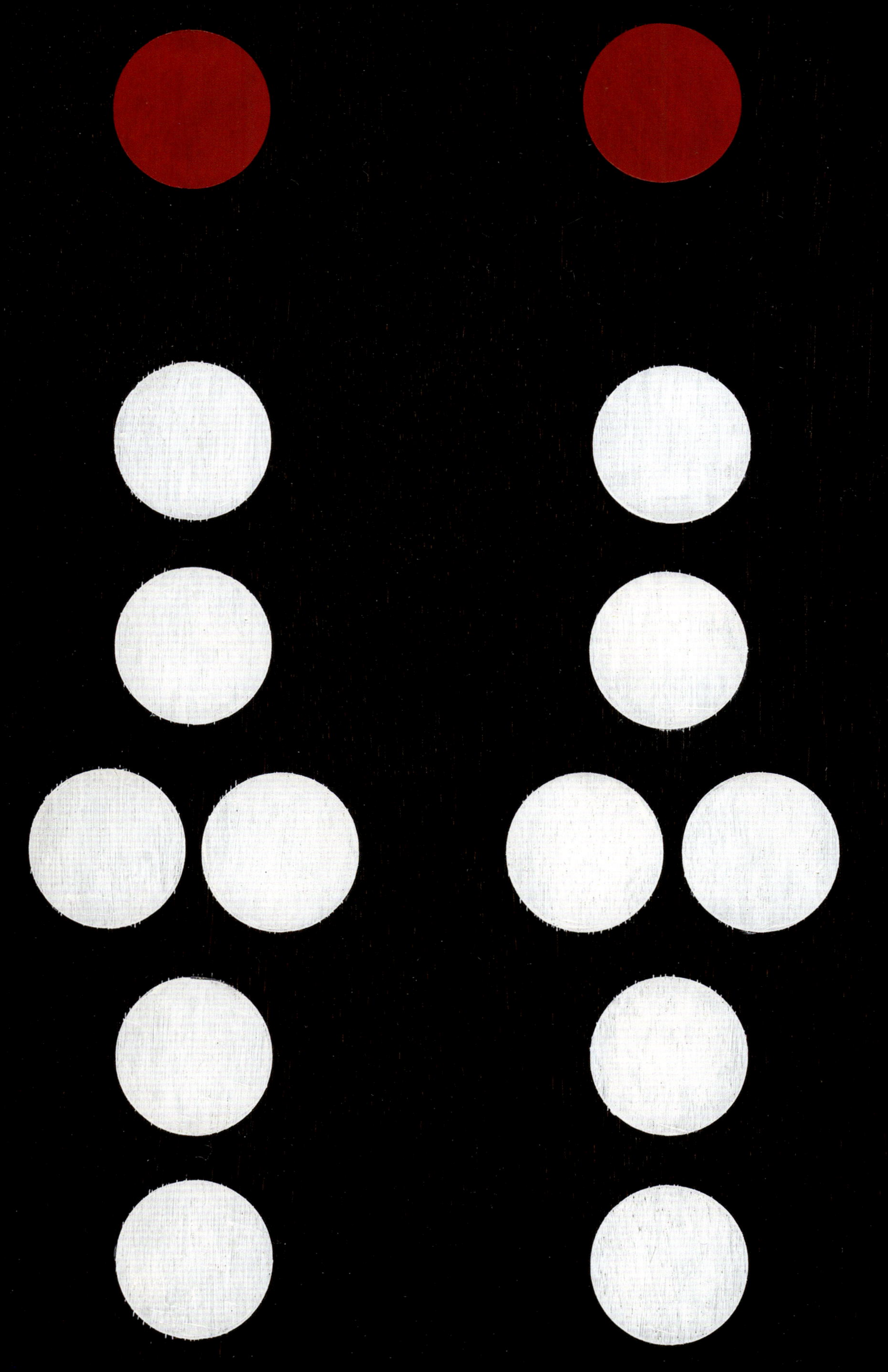

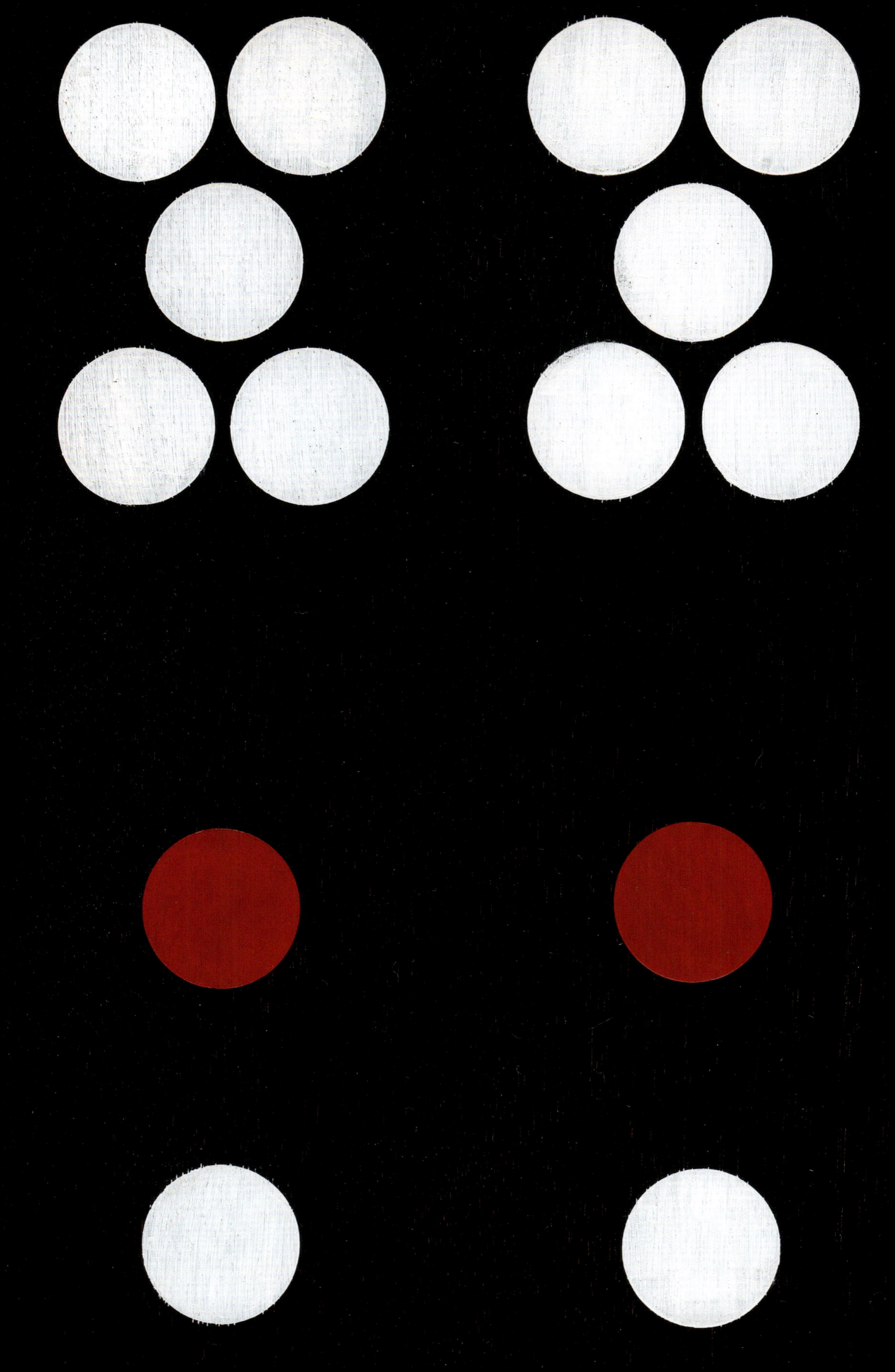

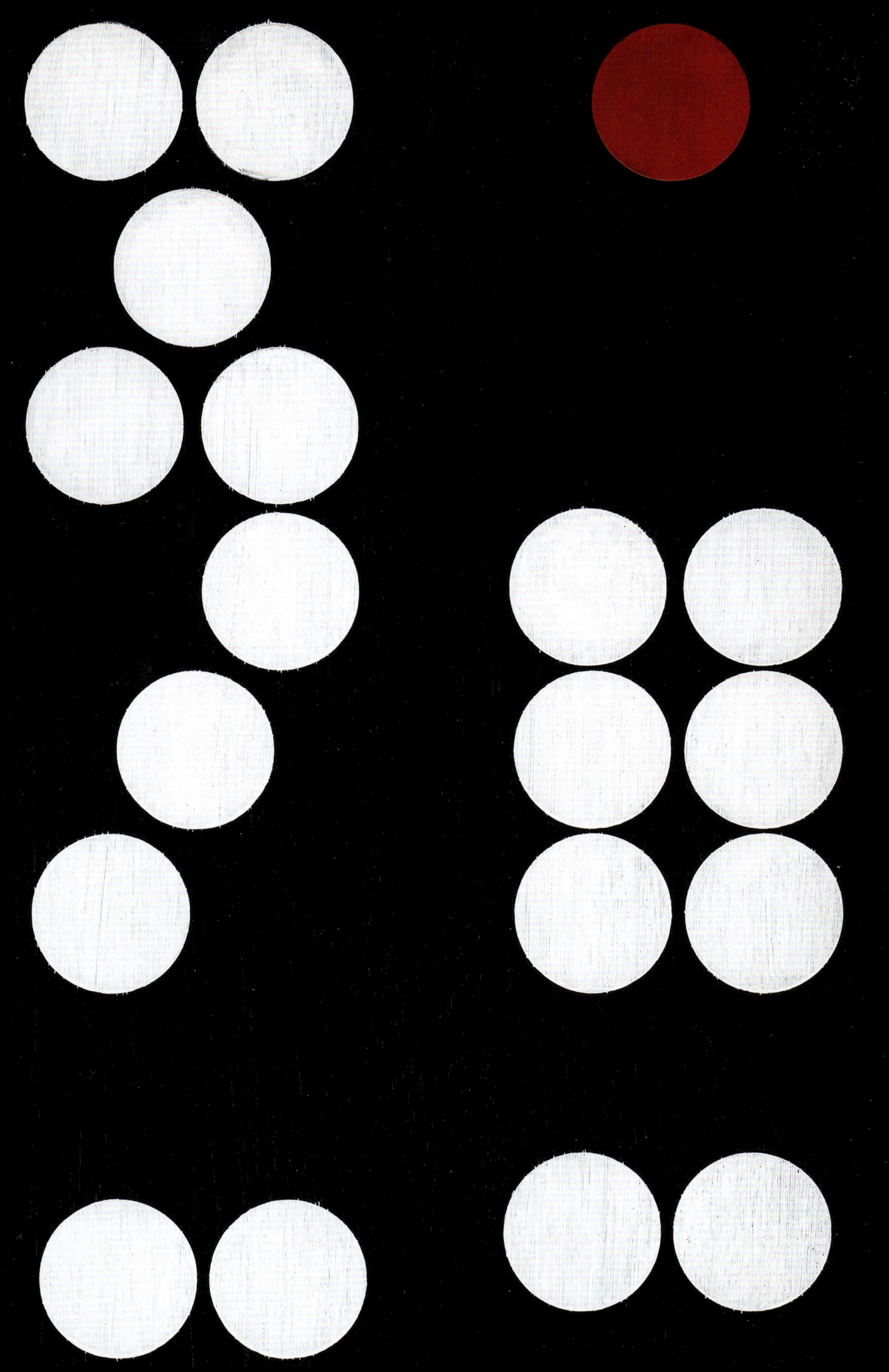

After Feininger

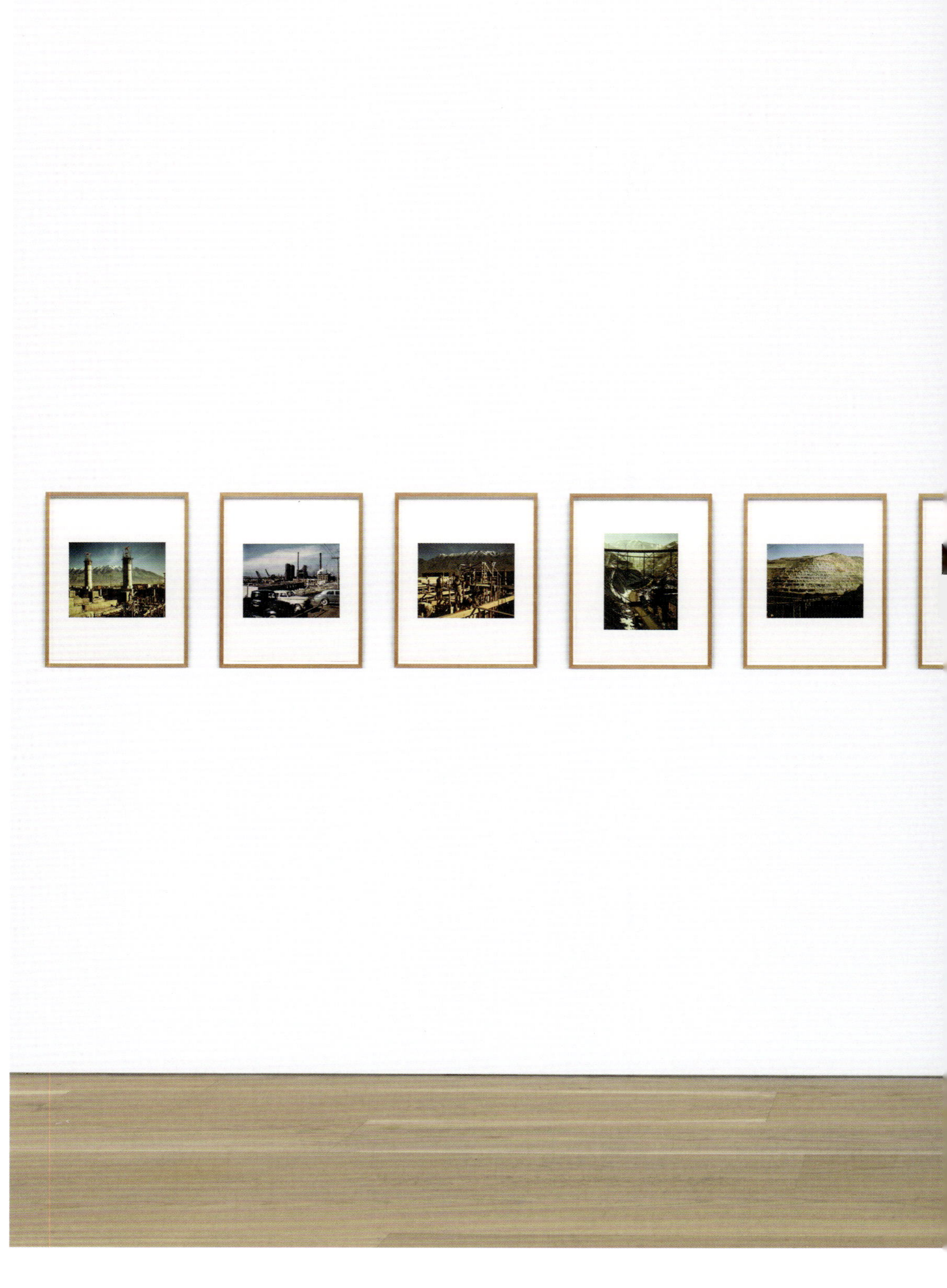

  Installation view, *After Feininger: 1–11*, 2021

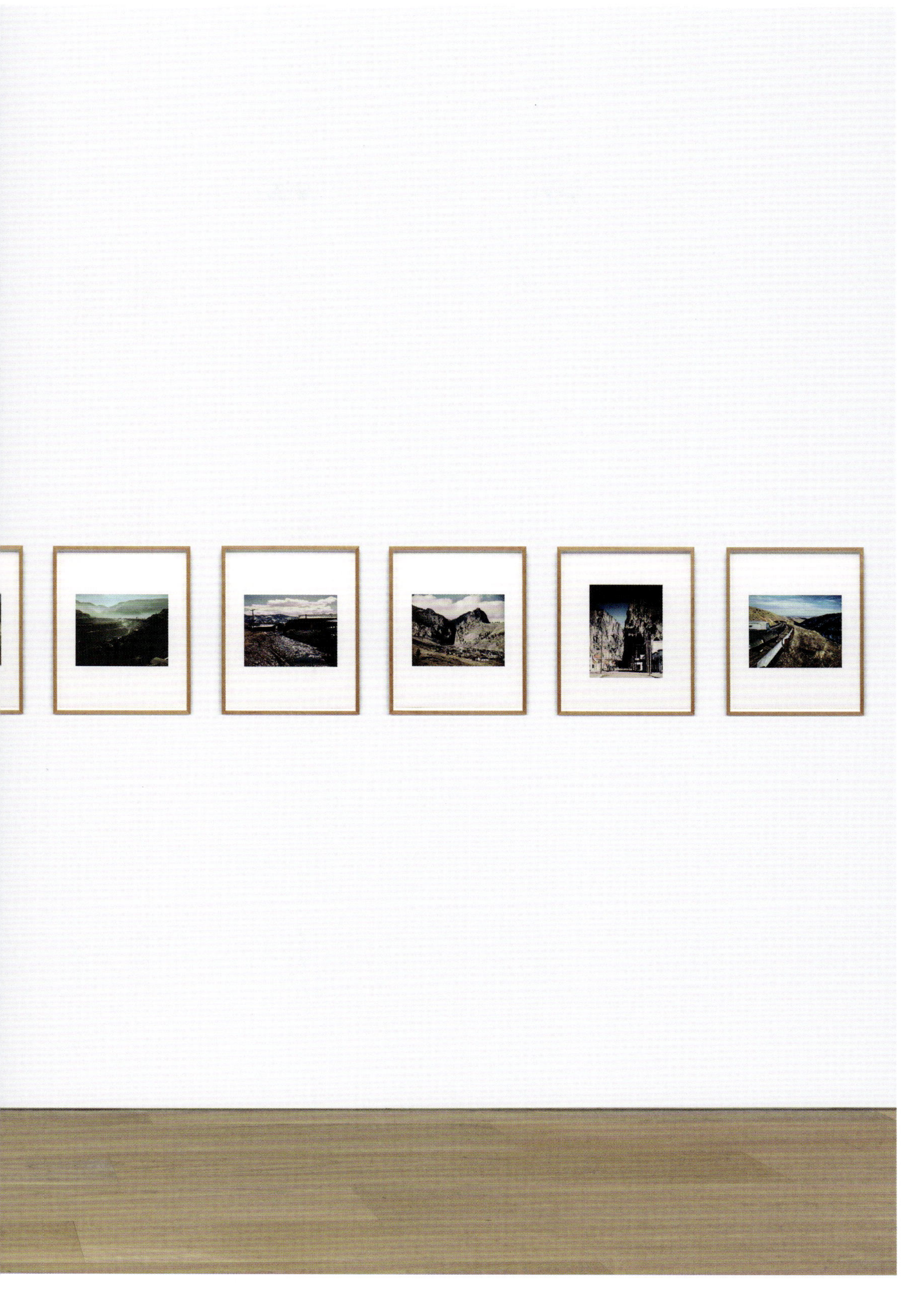

After Feininger: 1–11, 2021
Eleven giclée inkjet prints
Each: 20 × 16 inches
50.8 × 40.6 cm

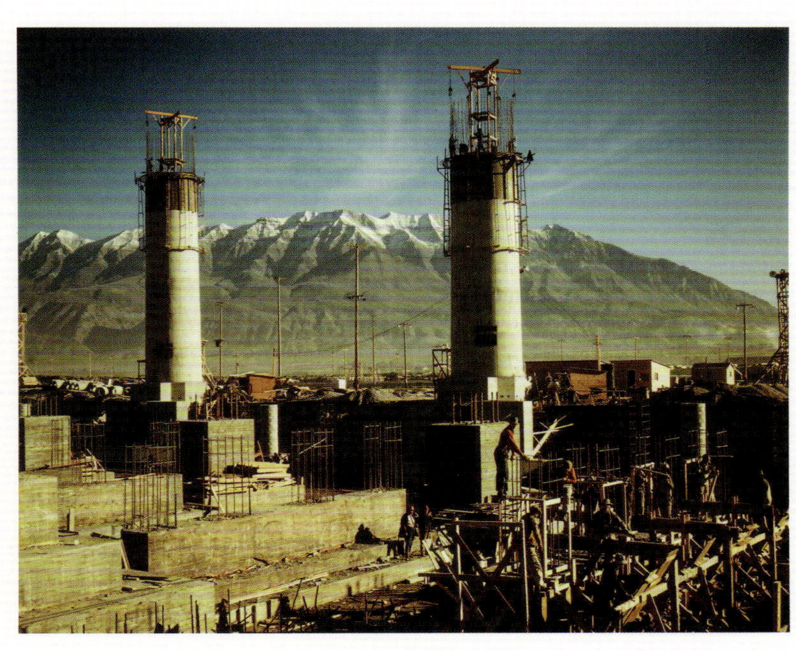

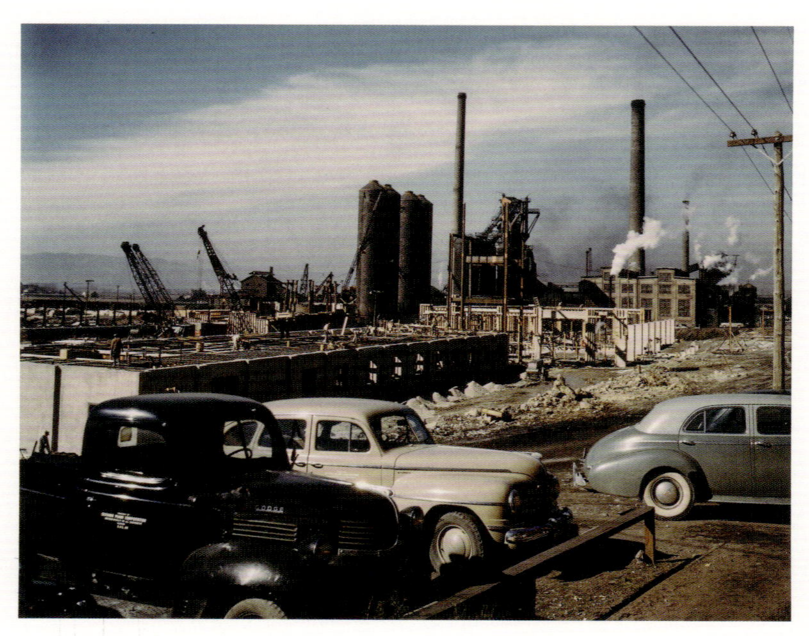

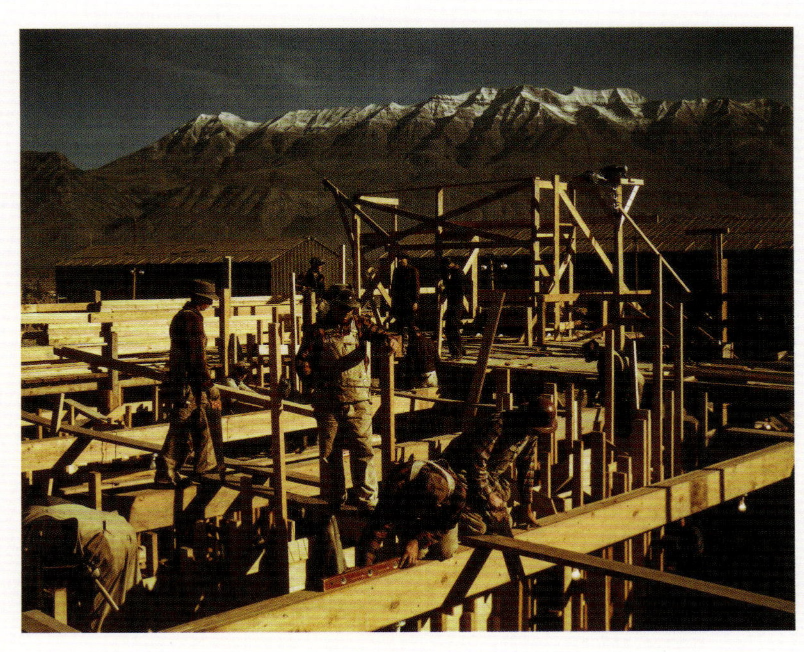

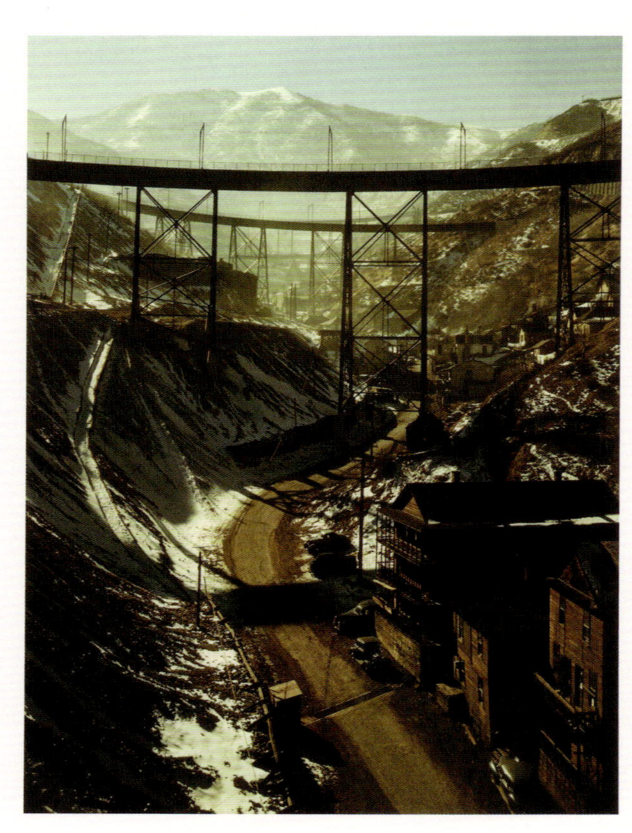

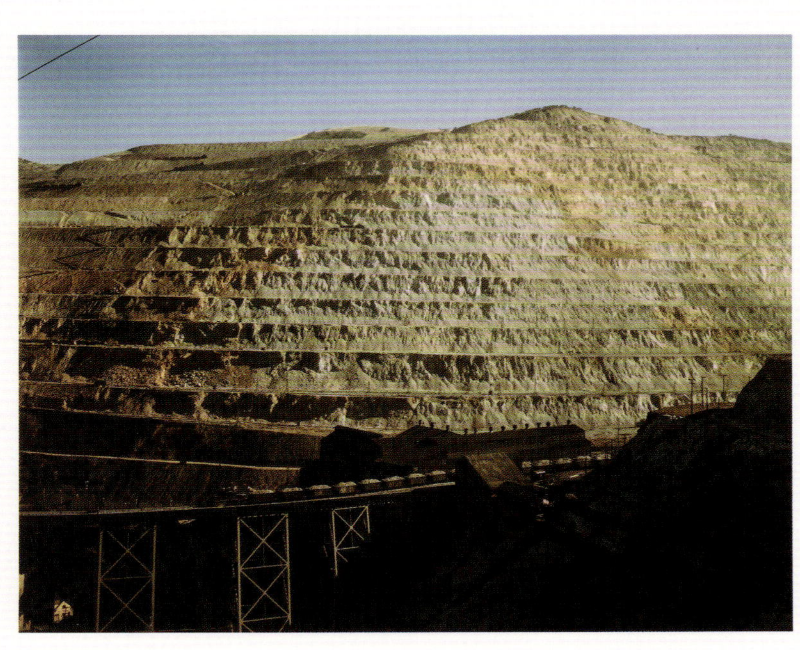

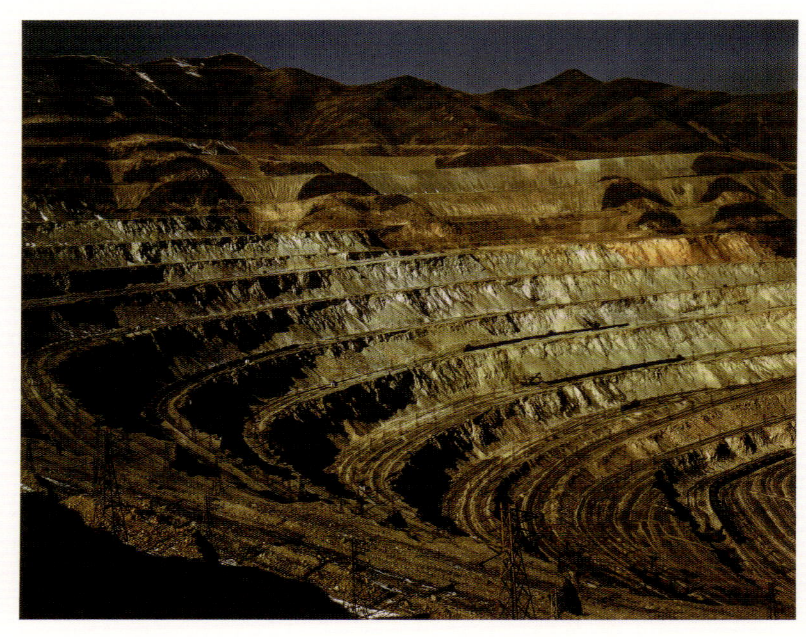

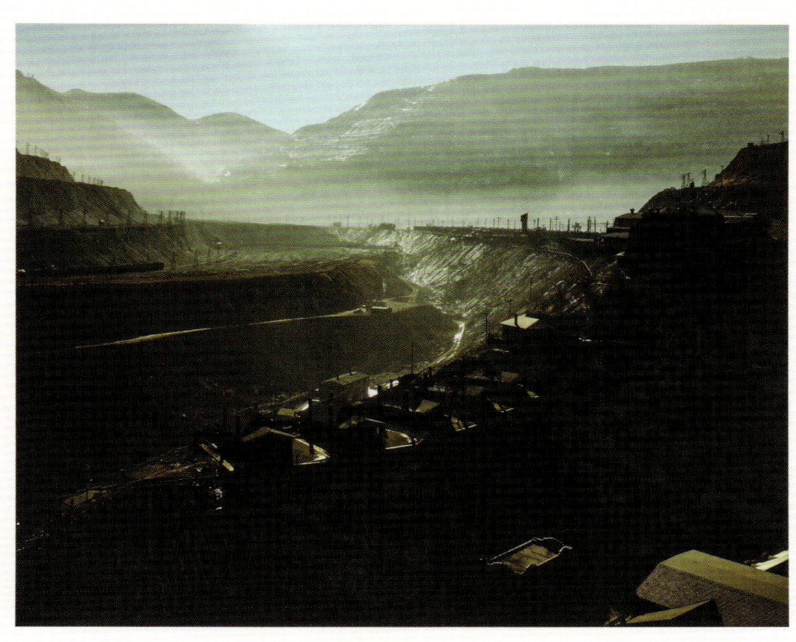

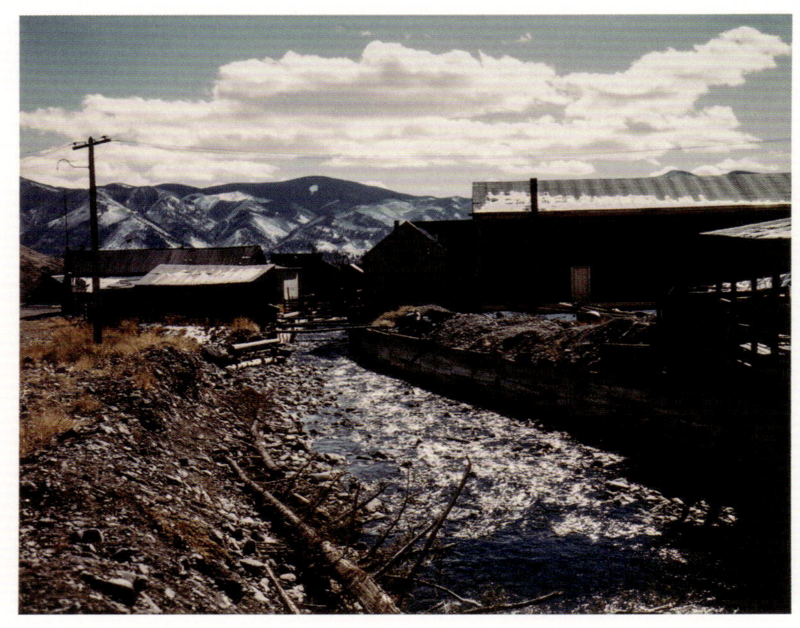

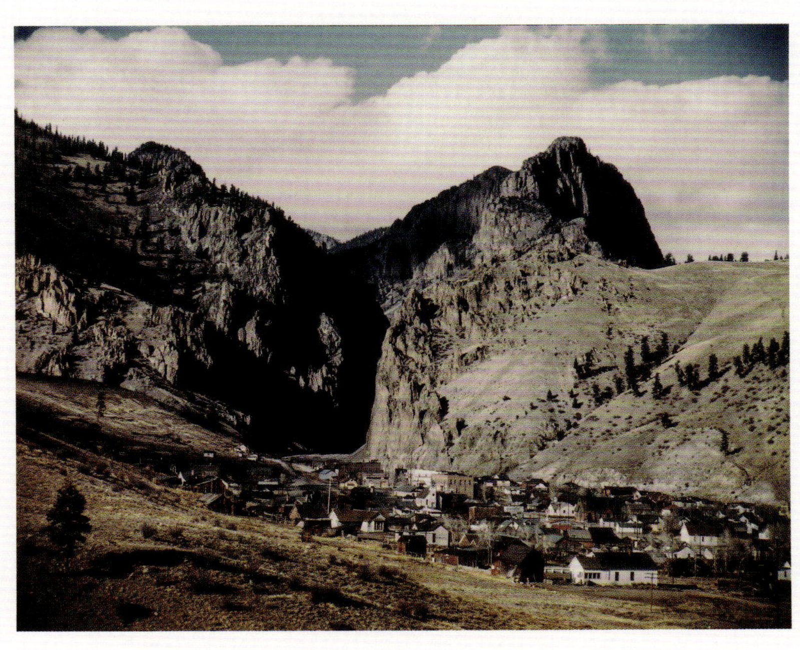

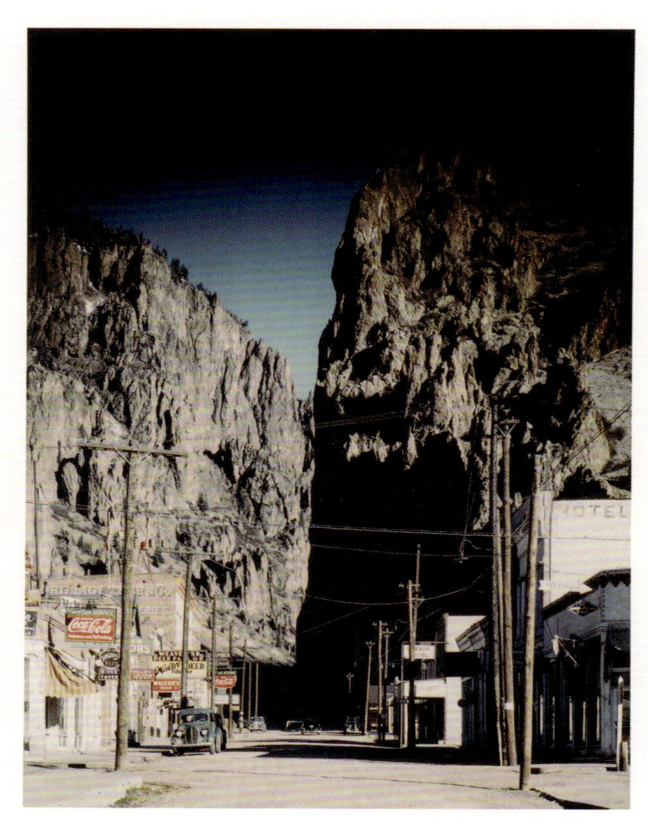

Coca-Cola
HOTEL

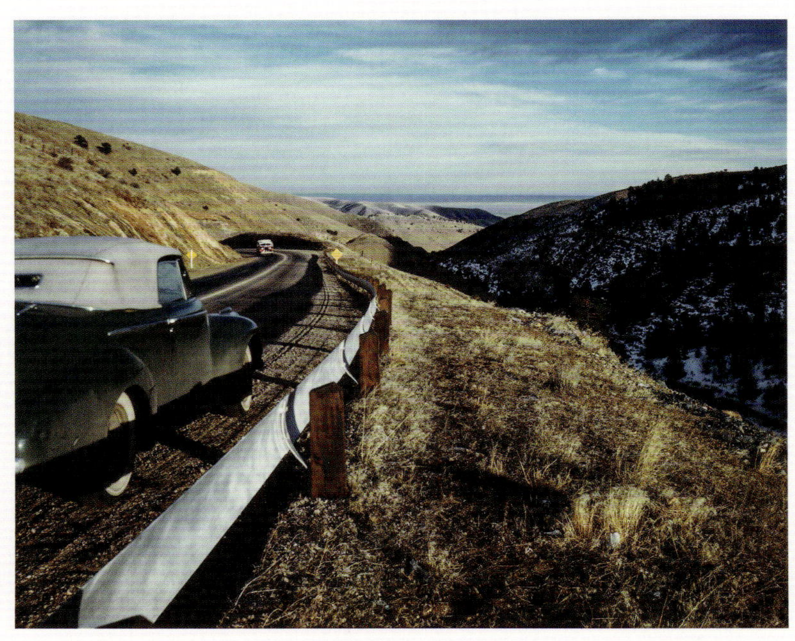

Sherrie Levine's singular and complex body of work engages many of the core tenets of postmodern art, in particular challenging notions of originality, authenticity, and identity. Born in 1947 in Hazleton, Pennsylvania, Levine studied at the University of Wisconsin–Madison, where she received her MFA in 1973.

In 2011, the Whitney Museum of American Art, New York, presented *MAYHEM*, a major exhibition of Levine's work spanning three decades. Levine's work has been the subject of solo exhibitions at prominent institutions worldwide, including Neues Museum, State Museum for Art and Design, Nuremberg (2016); Portland Art Museum, Oregon (2013); Museum Haus Lange, Krefeld, Germany (2010); San Francisco Museum of Modern Art (2009 and 1991); Georgia O'Keeffe Museum, Santa Fe, New Mexico (2007); Museum of Contemporary Art, Los Angeles (1995); The Menil Collection, Houston (1995); Portikus, Frankfurt (1994); Philadelphia Museum of Art (1993); Kunsthalle Zürich (1991); High Museum of Art, Atlanta (1988); Hirshhorn Museum and Sculpture Garden, Smithsonian Institution, Washington, DC (1988); and the Wadsworth Atheneum Museum of Art, Hartford, Connecticut (1987).

Work by the artist is held in international museum collections, including the Art Institute of Chicago; Centre Georges Pompidou, Paris; Hirshhorn Museum and Sculpture Garden, Smithsonian Institution, Washington, DC; Institute of Contemporary Art, Boston; Los Angeles County Museum of Art; Louisiana Museum of Modern Art, Humlebæk, Denmark; The Metropolitan Museum of Art, New York; The Museum of Modern Art, New York; The National Museum of Art, Osaka; San Francisco Museum of Modern Art; Solomon R. Guggenheim Museum, New York; Tate, London; and the Whitney Museum of American Art, New York. Levine lives and works in New York.

Larry List is a New York–based writer and curator. He is a contributor to the Man Ray catalogue raisonné, and his essays have appeared in a range of publications, including *Duchamp/Man Ray/Picabia*, *Transformer: The Work of Glenn Kaino*, *Takako Saito: Dreams to Do*, *Jan Fabre: Oro Rosso*, and *ViralNet*. His curatorial projects include *The Imagery of Chess Revisited*, *Skin Trade*, *John Cage & Glenn Kaino: Pieces & Performances*, *Xanti Schawinsky: Beyond the Bauhaus*, *Found Language*, and *Man Ray & Sherrie Levine: A Dialogue Through Objects, Images & Ideas*.

Jeanne Siegel was an influential writer, art critic, curator, and educator. She edited and contributed to numerous art journals and was the author of *Artwords: Discourse on the 60s and 70s*, *Art Talk: The Early 80s*, and *Painting After Pollock: Structures of Influence*. She served as the chair of the art history department at the School of Visual Arts, New York, from 1975 to 2000 and as the chair of the undergraduate fine arts department from 1976 to 2005. Siegel passed away in 2013.

Acknowledgments

David Zwirner wishes to thank Sherrie Levine, without whom this exhibition and catalogue would not have been possible, as well as Christopher D'Amelio and Leo Xu for their close collaboration and support. Special thanks are due to Joe Montgomery. We are especially grateful to Larry List for his illuminating text.

Thank you also to Beth Carpenter and to Rebecca Ashby-Colón, Paul Au, Claire Borre, Elizabeth Brannan-Williams, Alex Casto, Susan Cernek, Nadia Chan, Leanna Chen, Chantal Cheung, Allison Chipak, Anna Drozda, Jacob Ewert, Joanna Fiorentino, Richard Gamble, Anne-Claire Giraudon, Doro Globus, Elizabeth Gordon, Guo Juan, Collin Hatton, Tong Hu, Tony Huang, Maris Hutchinson, Claudia Ip, Tam Jumbala, Hope Kang, Susi Kenna, Michelle Kim, Tiffany Kok, Joe Lam, Celine Lau, Cicada Lee, Tiffany Leung, Shu Ming Lim, Thomas Ling, Louis Lu, Julia Lukacher, Kerry McFate, Clive Murphy, Jaime Schwartz, Molly Stein, Virginia Stroh, Galuh Sukardi, Kiko Tse, Ken Tsui, Ella Viscardi, Ernest Wan, Iona Whittaker, Chris Wu, Bess Yung, Rhys Ziemba, Lucas Zwirner, and all the staff at David Zwirner.

Published by David Zwirner
Books on the occasion of

*Sherrie Levine:
Hong Kong Dominoes*
David Zwirner
5–6/F, H Queen's
80 Queen's Road Central
Hong Kong
September 4–October 13,
2021

David Zwirner Books
529 West 20th Street
2nd Floor
New York, New York 10011
+1 212 727 2070
davidzwirnerbooks.com

Managing Director:
Doro Globus
Editorial Director:
Lucas Zwirner
Sales and Distribution
Manager: Molly Stein

Editor: Elizabeth Gordon
Photography Coordinators:
Rebecca Ashby-Colón,
Allison Chipak
Proofreader: Anna Drozda

Design: Chris Wu,
Ella Viscardi, Wkshps
Production Manager:
Paul Au, Gray Balance
Studio Limited
Color Separations:
Paul Au, Gray Balance
Studio Limited
Printing: Asia One,
Hong Kong

Typeface: Styrene B
Paper: Kinmari Matt EX,
157 gsm

Publication © 2021
David Zwirner Books
"Sherrie Levine: Take a
Picture to Make a Picture"
© 2021 Larry List
"After Sherrie Levine" ©
1985 Jeanne Siegel and
Sherrie Levine. Reprinted
with permission of the
Estate of Jeanne Siegel
All artwork © 2021
Sherrie Levine

"After Sherrie Levine"
was first published in *Arts
Magazine* in June 1985.
Slight adjustments were
made to spelling for this
publication.

Photography
pp. 5, 54–55, 56–57,
58–59, 60–61, 62–63,
64–65, 66–67, 68–69,
70–71, 72–73, 74–75,
76–77, 80–81, 82–83:
Maris Hutchinson
pp. 8, 9, 10, 11, 12, 13, 14, 15,
16, 17, 18, 19, 20, 21, 22, 23,
24, 25: Dan Bradica
pp. 46–47, 48–49, 84, 85,
86–87, 93, 94, 95, 96, 97,
98, 99, 100, 101, 102, 103:
Kerry McFate

Distributed in the United
States and Canada by
Simon & Schuster, Inc.
1230 Avenue of the Americas
New York, New York 10020
simonandschuster.com

Distributed outside the
United States and Canada by
Thames & Hudson, Ltd.
181A High Holborn
London WC1V 7QX
thamesandhudson.com

ISBN 978-1-64423-063-3

Library of Congress Control
Number: 2021912643

Printed in Hong Kong

Cover: *Hong Kong Dominoes:
1–12*, 2017 (detail)

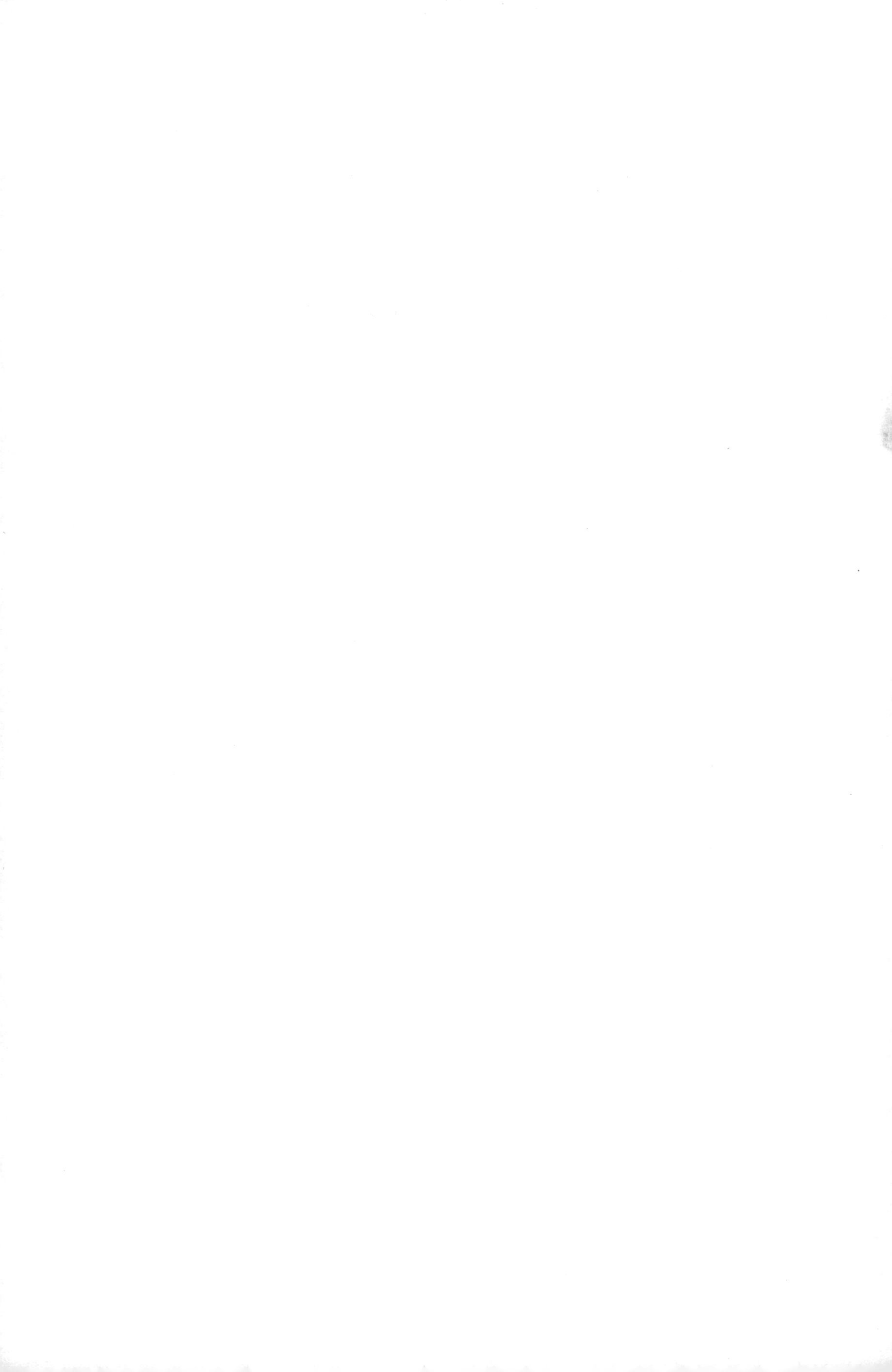